Sri Aurobindo

The Revolution of India

Luc Venet

Works of Sri Aurobindo are quoted with the permission of the Sri Aurobindo Ashram Trust, Pondicherry, India, which has also permitted the reproduction of the photographs of Sri Aurobindo.

Cover design: Vincent Jan Wolterbeek
Artwork: Paolo Tommasi

Copyright @ 2017 Luc Venet

Contents

PART ONE
Jnana – Knowledge

CHAPTER I
1893 | Arrival   11
Apollo Bunder, Bombay – English Scholarship – At Baroda Palace – Gentleman and Native – First Chronicles – The Being of Light – Gandhi

CHAPTER II
1894-1899 | At Home in India   31
Family Visit – Bankim, Ramakrishna, Vivekananda – Life in Baroda – A Program of Revolution

CHAPTER III
1901-1903 | Engagement   52
Famine – Marriage – India's Solitary Tapasya – First Samiti – Preparations for the Rebellion – The Throne of Solomon

CHAPTER IV
1903 – 1906 | Partition of Bengal   73
Menace over Bengal – "Build a Temple" – Three Cases of Madness – Boycott and Swadeshi – Call to Passive Resistance – National College of Bengal – The New Party

PART TWO
Karma – Works

CHAPTER V
1906 | Bande Mataram — 103
Yugantar, a Singular Newspaper – The Stormy Barisal Conference – National College – Temple of Kali – A Political Maelstrom – The Bande Mataram

CHAPTER VI
1906-1907 | Outbreak of Hostilities — 121
Calcutta Congress – Divide and Conquer – Doctrine of Passive Resistance – Communal Violence – Young Revolutionary Brother

CHAPTER VII
1907 | Repression — 136
The Bande Mataram and the Virtues of the Warrior – Repression Against the Swadeshi – The Trial of The Bande Mataram

CHAPTER VIII
1907-1908 | The Breakup — 148
Head of the Nationalist Movement – The Surat Congress: The Breakup – Nirvana – Inspired Political Appeals

CHAPTER IX
1908 | The Bhagavad Gita — 161
Silence – Militant Violence – Karmayoga and the War of Kurukshetra – Violence and Destruction – Fatal Explosion

PART THREE
Bhakti – Love

CHAPTER X

1908-1909 | Alipore   177

Prison – Lessons of God – Krishna – The Trial – Silence and Yoga – Executions – Spiritual Explorations – Facing Trial – The High Court of History

CHAPTER XI

1909-1910 | The Karmayogin   209

Slackening of the Nationalist Movement – Uttarpara Speech – The Karmayogin – The Two Ends of Existence – Menace to Freedom – Rise of Terrorism – Last Involvements – Political Swamp – The Noose Tightens – Standing Aside – Taking Stock – Chandernagore

CHAPTER XII

1910 | Departure   247

In the Steps of the Vedic Rishis – Last days in Chandernagore – Pondicherry

Postscript   258

About the Author   263

References   264

PART ONE

Jnana – Knowledge

Spirituality is indeed the master-key of the Indian mind; the sense of the infinite is native to it. India saw from the beginning that life cannot be rightly seen in the sole light, cannot be perfectly lived in the sole power of its externalities... She saw too that man has the power of exceeding himself, of becoming himself more entirely and profoundly than he is... she saw that there were ranges of life beyond our life, ranges of mind beyond our present mind and above these she saw the splendours of the spirit...

                Sri Aurobindo, *The Renaissance in India*, 1918.

CHAPTER I

1893

Arrival

Apollo Bunder, Bombay

From the quarterdeck, Aurobindo contemplated the heaving mass of the ocean. Throughout the night he had been searching the brooding darkness. At long last a pale line ruptured the horizon. India was drawing near. To the pulsating rhythm of the engines, the steamer headed towards the growing light. Burning off the last shreds of morning mist, an enormous sun soared into the sky, revealing the outlines of a city. The day dawned on Bombay.

Aurobindo Ghose was twenty. He came from England, where he had spent thirteen years steeped in Western classical culture. An accomplished scholar in Graeco-Latin tradition, he read the major authors of European literature in their original languages, spoke refined English and wrote in an elegant style, which had earned him praise from his professors at Cambridge. Even his attire was that of a Western gentleman.

Somewhat unsteadily, after a month at sea, he stepped ashore onto the Apollo Bunder amidst the hustle and bustle of a colourful crowd. No one awaited him. He made his way through the jumble of porters and zigzagging hand-carts, children and dogs, heavily laden donkeys and placid cows, captivated by the exuberance of India. As his senses drank in the flood of clamour and colours, a strange sensation came over him. An immense calm flowed into his entire being. No more thoughts, no more emotions, no bodily awareness – all inexplicably dissolved in an extraordinary silence. He now walked mechanically through the crowd, disconnected, as in a void, his body a speck in infinity. Boundaries abolished, each object, each living creature, each movement came alive in this greater Self – the whole world breathed within him. He surrendered, abandoning himself to the fullness of the moment, to the Light penetrating his being....

*A momentless immensity pure and bare,
I stretch to an eternal everywhere.*[1]

Nothing had prepared the young Aurobindo for such an experience, even though, only a few weeks earlier, he had happened upon a text of which every word had remained engraved in his mind:

It stirs and it stirs not; it is far, and likewise near. It is inside of all this, and it is outside of all this.

And he who beholds all beings in the Self, and the Self in all beings, he never turns away from it.

When to a man who understands, the Self has become all things, what sorrow, what trouble can there be to him who once beheld that unity?[2]

These three verses referred to the *Atman*, or transcendent Self. Aurobindo connected them to the mute magnificence still pervading his being. Yes, inside of all things... yes, the unity of All....

In England, intrigued by these lines, he had attempted to "comprehend" this *Atman*, the cornerstone of India's ancestral explanation of the universe. He remembered an annotation made by the English translator, an Oxford professor named Max Müller: "Beyond the ego, with all its accidents and limitations, such as sex, sense, language, country, and religion, the ancient sages of India perceived, from a very early time, the Atman or Self, independent of all such accidents."[3]

His steps led him to the train station, bringing him back to ordinary consciousness. Could it be that he had experienced the revelation of this *Atman* on which the ancient Yogis of the *Upanishads** had based their philosophical system? Had he, if only fleetingly, caught a glimpse of his ancestors' metaphysical wisdom?

Aurobindo will not breathe a word about what he felt upon his arrival in Bombay. On this 6 February 1893, he did not know that this was only the first of the spiritual

---
*   Written between five to eight centuries B.C., the *Upanishads* are one of the major metaphysical texts of India's culture.

experiences the future held for him. But 56 years later, he would write:

> Since I set foot on Indian soil on the Apollo Bunder in Bombay, I began to have spiritual experiences, but these were not divorced from this world but had an inner and intimate bearing on it, such as a feeling of the Infinite pervading material space and the Immanent inhabiting material objects and bodies. At the same time, I found myself entering supraphysical worlds and planes with influences and an effect from them upon the material plane, so I could make no sharp divorce or irreconcilable opposition between what I have called the two ends of existence and all that lies between them.[4]

Arriving at Bombay Central Station he boarded a train to Baroda. The Maharajah awaited him.

English Scholarship

Thirteen years earlier, Krishna Ghose, a medical graduate from Aberdeen University in Scotland, had sent his three sons to study in England, as he himself had done. The youngest, Aurobindo, was only seven years old.

A native of Bengal, where he held the post of medical officer in charge of Rangpur District, Dr Ghose admired the British system to the extent of banning the use of Bengali in his household in favour of steeping his family in English culture. "We know the English are a superior race and can teach us much,"[5] he proclaimed. This was the time of the great Darwinian debate on *The Origin of Species*,* and the doctor's medical education impelled him to champion a world governed by reason. Through a friend, he had come into contact with an Anglican clergyman in Manchester, William Drewett, who had agreed to take in his three sons and to guide their education.

Swarnalotta and Krishna Ghose in England with their three sons and little Sarojini. Aurobindo is in the front row to the right.

Dr. Ghose accompanied his sons to England with Swarnalotta, his wife, who suffered from a mental

---

* In 1859, in writing *The Origin of Species*, Darwin had call into question the evolutionary origin of man. His second major work, *The Descent of Man* (1871), had just been published.

disorder. He took advantage of their stay in London to have her seen to by a neurologist.

In 1879, despite the Suez Canal, it still took four weeks to travel to England. The doctor escorted his sons to Drewett's home in Manchester and almost immediately turned around to go back to India, leaving Swarnalotta in the hands of the specialist. There in England, in January 1880, she gave birth to their fourth son, Barin, whose revolutionary impetuosity would play a leading role in Aurobindo's life and in the future emancipation of India.

Before leaving, the doctor wanted to capture the image of his family. The photo shows a man with calm determination standing between his two eldest sons, who look somewhat like frightened fawns, a chubby Sarojini sitting on her mother's lap, and in the foreground, seated with his hands on his knees, seven-year-old Aurobindo, whose eyes shine with an intense curiosity.

In this bleak suburb of the largest English industrial centre, one can imagine the three young boys concentrating for hours on the five Latin declensions, between the ancient world which Pastor Drewett tried to bring to life in their heads and the new world opening before their eyes. Through the window, they could see the grey smoke of the smelting furnaces that obscured the skyline and hear the roar of the boilers and sharp metallic clanging.

After two years of this austere regime, the two older boys were ready to enter grammar school. Aurobindo, who had just turned nine, continued to receive private lessons: Latin and history with the pastor, French, geography and arithmetic with his wife.

However, he had a clear preference for poetry. At age ten, he fell in love with Shelley, who inspired him to compose (later to be published in a local Manchester magazine) his first poem, *Light*, modelled on the versification of *The Cloud*. Another work of Shelley's drew his special attention, *The Revolt of Islam*, in which two young heroes fomented a bloodless coup against the Sultan of the Ottoman Empire. Not formulated in the terms of a political awakening, this was nevertheless the dawn of an interest in subjects that spoke of transforming the world.

Aurobindo fulfilled his father's expectations. At seventeen, he won prizes in classical and modern literature and ranked first at the entrance examination for King's College, Cambridge. He became a "gentleman," the iconic status that English tradition confers upon its elite. In addition, he was awarded a scholarship to study for the Indian Civil Service (ICS), the academic credentials required for entering the government bureaucracy. For two years, he explored the jungle of legal doctrines in force in India. From the Code of Justinian to Jeremy Bentham's *An Introduction to the Principles of Morals and Legislation*, not to mention Hindu law, Muslim law and British India's Penal Code, nothing must elude the erudition of the future administrators of the Empire. He even attended John Neville Keynes's classes on political economy.

His thirst for learning seemed insatiable and his curiosity boundless. He devoured French and English novels and European history. Indifferent to formal philosophy, he did not share in the enthusiasm of his time for Hegel and Kant but read Plato, whose *Republic* and *Symposium* he placed among humanity's "highest points of thought and literature."[6] At eighteen, he was so impressed by these two works that he began writing, in the Platonic mode,

The Harmony of Virtue, "an explanation of the cosmos on the foundation of the principle of Beauty and Harmony."[7] His interest in Plato predisposed him to a reasonable agnosticism.

While he successfully passed the academic tests for the entrance examination to the ICS, he neglected one last formality: to display his skill in horsemanship, and consequently he was denied final admittance. His influential friends rallied. "That a man of this calibre should be lost to the Indian Government merely because he failed in sitting on a horse or did not keep an appointment appears to me, I confess, a piece of official short-sightedness which it would be hard to beat,"[8] wrote one of his tutors at Cambridge. The Secretary of State for India himself was urged to intercede in his favour, but he ratified the ICS decision by pronouncing that "no candidate ought to be allowed to go to India who cannot ride."[9]

Deep down, however, Aurobindo was not displeased with this setback. For months, he had developed an instinctive aversion to the administrative system introduced under British rule. He could not see himself adopting the lifestyle expected of his prospective colleagues in the Indian Civil Service. His disqualification exempted him from having to reject the Service, which his family would not have allowed. For the first time in his life, Aurobindo had challenged paternal wishes.

It was Henry Cotton, a member of the ICS and long-time friend of the Ghose family, who found a way out of the predicament. Having learned that the Maharajah of Baroda was stopping over in London, he solicited an interview for Aurobindo. The Maharajah received the young man and, seizing upon an opportunity to ensure the qualifications of an ICS student without having to pay the high price of a graduate, he offered to hire him in the administration of his principality. The proposal suited Aurobindo's inclination, as he presumed the Baroda environment to be less rigid than the British administration. The modest salary offer (Rs 200 per month) could not dampen the hope of a promising future.

At Baroda Palace

India was under British domination. In 1858, following the Sepoy Mutiny, the government of Queen Victoria had taken the reins from the East India Company, a commercial enterprise which had run India as its private property for two and a half centuries. India had become the British Raj and Queen Victoria, the "Empress of India." To control a territory ten times the size of England and populated by three hundred million people, the British had divided it into "presidencies" (large provinces), administered by British-appointed governors, under the supervision of a Governor-General, or Viceroy, who shared the responsibility of running the country with the Secretary of State in Westminster. But some six hundred princes and maharajahs, who had pledged allegiance to Victoria in matters of defence and foreign policy, had retained control of their princely estates.

Baroda was the capital of one of those semi-independent enclaves. Three hundred miles north of Bombay, this principality of about a thousand square miles, headed by Maharajah Sayaji Roa Gaekwar III, was one of the Empire's most prosperous. Educated from childhood by

English tutors, the sovereign was known for his liberalism. His reign (1875-1939) is regarded as the Golden Age of Baroda. It was during his third trip to Europe that the thirty-year-old monarch had met Aurobindo.

Four times the size of Buckingham Palace, in the middle of a five-hundred-acre park, the residence of the Maharajah stood like an apparition worthy of *The Thousand and One Nights*.

In a recent publication, Gayatri Devi, the Maharajah's granddaughter, describes the life of her brothers and sisters in this thousand-room fairyland edifice.[10] "Lakshmi Vilas was a huge building surrounded by marble verandas with scalloped arches, supported by arrays of thin columns. The interior of the palace was a curious blend, partly Victorian, partly traditional Indian, with here and there touches of English or French craftsmanship. Persian rugs ran along endless corridors.

Lakshmi Vilas Palace

The salons were crowded with French furniture, photographs in silver frames, ornaments and trinkets placed on low tables. [...] Contrasting with our impeccable bearing and the courtesy everyone extended towards us, long-tailed monkeys moved about everywhere. It took very little to make them angry, and they would chase after us through the corridors, shrieking and snarling in a terrifying way."

The Maharajah, who had learned to rule his people under British tutelage, challenged his new appointee's character. Initially assigned to the Settlement Department, Aurobindo would spend the first year navigating the labyrinth of land assessment, before being transferred to the Revenue Department, where he became acquainted with the tax code and the intricacies of tax collection. He learned enough Gujarati (the language of the principality) and Marathi (used at court) to communicate easily with everyone. It is only after three years of this apprenticeship that the Maharajah entrusted him with tasks more attuned to his skills.

Fortunately, his stay in England had taught him detachment, and he possessed a surprising ability to disengage himself through mental concentration; to this end, his work environment was the perfect training ground.

Despite the monotony of his work, every moment strengthened his conviction that he had made the right choice in turning down the material advantages of a Western career: here was the appointed place of his destiny, bringing out "a natural attraction to Indian culture and ways of life and a temperamental feeling and preference for all that is Indian."[11] He adopted Indian dress habits, and although during the day he donned the obligatory three-piece suit, in private he wore a white dhoti,*

---
* Large rectangular piece of cotton fabric skilfully wrapped to cover the body from the waist down

along with a coarse Ahmedabad cotton shawl and old-fashioned slippers with upturned toes.

In his spare time he wrote or resumed the study of Sanskrit he had begun in England as an autodidact by reading the *Mahabharata*, the great epic text of Indian mythology. To daily translate some forty lines of this monumental poem was demanding, but after a month of practice, he felt ready to tackle the more esoteric Sanskrit of the *Upanishads*.* He aspired to explore the original treatises of ancient India, to trace the source of their insight, to understand what ushered in this primaeval thought, "this true Being or true Substance,"[12] (in the words of the *Upanishads*).

Although his intellectual background favoured a relativistic reading of existence and while the Industrial Revolution exploded in feverish expectations in the world around him, Aurobindo longed for some unalterable course of life, an innermost absolute.

His experience in Bombay remained vivid. He could recall the sovereign state of awareness beyond all contingency, outside the world's mental or sensory restrictive experience. To his astonishment, the stamp of the hushed silence had lingered within him: some indefinable presence remained in the background of all his activities. Whenever he checked his thoughts and withdrew within himself, the silence came back: a bedrock of unshakeable, exquisite peace, an impersonal stillness that dissolved the world's agitation in its unassailable blankness. He had grown accustomed to flowing into this space in the midst

---

* Excerpts of Sri Aurobindo's commentaries and translation of the *Upanishads* are found in the Appendix.

of his work, always emerging from these moments of disconnection with renewed energy.

Yet Aurobindo had no plan to turn to spiritual practices. Outside his work, his mind was taken up by poetry and by what seemed the extreme opposite of poetry: politics.

Gentleman and Native

Aurobindo's political awareness had developed during his stay in England in part due to his father's correspondence. Over the years, Krishna Ghose had ceased admiring the British system. He now called it "a heartless government", and he incorporated in his letters clippings from *The Bengalee* chronicling mistreatment of Indians by the British authorities.

At Cambridge there had been no question of mistreatment but of affinity and community of interest. However, the sports, activities and mindset of his English classmates did not appeal to the young Indian student. Aurobindo remained courteous but at a distance, and he spontaneously chose his companions among his compatriots. He thus befriended Keshav Deshpande, with whom he will share his revolutionary ideals. In London the two friends had keenly followed the repeated failures of Prime Minister Gladstone in introducing the Irish Home Rule in Parliament. Aurobindo's sympathy went rather to Charles Stewart Parnell, the Irish Nationalist leader and former Cantabrigian, whose courage and convictions drew admiration even from the British Parliament's benches.

(After Parnell's death in 1891, he would dedicate two poems to his memory.)

Emerging from his reserve, the young Aurobindo began displaying his Nationalist feelings and delivering impassioned speeches at meetings of the Indian Majlis, a student organisation he headed for a time, before enlisting briefly in a "secret society", romantically called "Lotus and Dagger"....

Now back in India, he faced the drab reality of British occupation: the trivialities of the philistine and the hypocrisy of big business interests beneath the veneered politeness and calculated liberalism.

The English controlled the country with practically no use of force, but rather through tacit agreement. Some sort of hypnotic spell seemed to work its magic on Indian society, empowering fewer than 100 000 men from a distant island to impose their system on three hundred million individuals. For Aurobindo, this spell – "the artificial glare of English prestige,"[13] as he called it, – was the crux of the problem. His historical readings on revolutionary movements which resulted in establishing a nation (from Joan of Arc to the American Revolution to the Unification of Italy) had taught him that it would be futile to expect a radical transformation of society to emerge from parliamentary proceedings. He was silently contemplating the only prospect for a change – a forcible expulsion of the British – without knowing how this could come about.

In the government offices, where the Maharajah deliberately called him *Aurobindo Babu* because of his scholarship and Bengali origin, he became *Mister Aurobindo Ghose* to his colleagues. However, to the English, despite his impeccable accent, he remained a "native". His status as a gentleman, which had transcended race in London and Cambridge, seemingly vanished after crossing an invisible frontier at the Suez Canal. Here a gulf divided the two races.

First Chronicles

A few months after arriving in Baroda, an opportunity arose to make his voice heard. Keshav Deshpande, his comrade from Cambridge, who had been appointed editor-in-chief of the *Indu Prakash,* a Bombay literary and political weekly, suggested he write an article. Aurobindo accepted, even though his association with the Maharajah forced him to write anonymously.

The British Parliament had just granted approval for the Indian Civil Service examination to be held simultaneously in England and in India. For an enthusiastic Indian press this measure was further proof of British benevolence. To the tide of euphoria, Aurobindo responded sarcastically: "This chorus of jubilant paeans arising from the Press, resembles nothing so much as the joyful chorus of ducks when the monsoon arrives." In reality, he pointed out, the vote in Parliament had been obtained by surprise, by the sole presence in the House of a handful of liberal members favourable to India, "but [it] no more expresses the real feeling of the English people than a decree of the Chinese Emperor would express it." Castigating a press that "seems eager to accept even the flimsiest excuse for deluding itself," he proceeded to give a rundown of the voting blocs and prevailing influences in the House of Commons, where India was chronically under-represented, before launching into an incisive indictment of his countrymen's attitude:

> We constantly find it asserted that the English are a just people and only require our case to be clearly stated in order to redress our grievances. It is more than time that some voice should be raised – even though it may be the voice of one crying in the wilderness – to tell the Press and the public that this is a grave and injurious delusion, which must be expunged from our minds if we would see things as they really are.... If we are indeed to renovate our country, we must no longer hold out supplicating hands to the English Parliament, like an infant crying to its nurse for a toy, but must recognise the hard truth that every nation must beat out its own path to salvation with pain and difficulty, and not rely on the tutelage of another.[14]

What a defiant voice for a twenty-year-old! Barely out of adolescence, he challenged his adult countrymen to confront their servitude and assume their manhood, urging them to break the yoke of their illusions. This first address to his country announced what will be the hallmark of his call: an imperative for emotional catharsis, the need to find the cause of the ills and their remedy in oneself. From what inner recesses did this young man draw this energy? What intuition, what wisdom was being expressed through one who shone such an unwavering light on the massive capitulation of his people?

Delighted with this first article, his friend Deshpande asked for more. A month later, Aurobindo submitted the beginning of a series of essays entitled "New Lamps for Old," devoted to examining the nature and workings of the *Indian National Congress*. Consisting of an Anglophile Indian elite, the Government-tolerated "Congress" was national only in name and popular only in the minds of its members. Conceived eight years earlier by its English founder, Allan Hume, as a "safety valve,"[15] it helped to channel the frustrations of the colonised without challenging the colonial system. It met every December to confirm the pre-eminence of the British system of government. Of the dozens of resolutions it had voted on, only one had elicited a tepid response from the authorities. Its yearly displays of pomposity were greeted with complete indifference by the Indian population.

Despite its obvious imperfections, the Congress was the only Indian political arena. It was the mind-set of its leading members – the party bosses who claimed an assumed liberalism – which precluded any likelihood of political emancipation. In his essays, Aurobindo emphasised the mimicry of their orientation and their deluded optimism in the British parliamentary system. To one of the leaders who referred to "the class" represented by Congress members as "the thinking portion of the population," he retorted:

> If I were asked to describe their class by a single name, I should not hesitate to call it our new middle class. For here too English goods have driven out native

goods: our society has lost its old landmarks and is being demarcated on the English model.[16]

Retracing the short history of the Congress from its inception and evoking the general disappointment caused by its inability to affirm itself as a credible political counterpart to the colonial authorities, Aurobindo argued that its activities can be summarised in just one word: failure. It was now high time that Indians should confront the problems besetting them and abandon their servility and naivety about the supposed selflessness of English politicians. Then he grew bolder:

> Now that I am compelled to handle my subject more intimately and with a firmer grasp, nothing but my deliberate conviction that it is quite imperative for someone to speak out, has at all persuaded me to continue. I say, of the Congress, then, this, – that its aims are mistaken, that the spirit in which it proceeds towards their accomplishment is not a spirit of sincerity and whole-heartedness, and that the methods it has chosen are not the right methods, and the leaders in whom it trusts, not the right sort of men to be leaders; – in brief, that we are at present the blind led, if not by the blind, at any rate by the one-eyed.[17]

The reaction would not be long in coming. No sooner was Aurobindo's text made public than one of the Congress leaders informed the publisher of the *Indu Prakash* that he would be prosecuted for sedition if future essays continued in the same vein. Deshpande asked the fiery writer to tone down his criticisms by coating them in "academia". Aurobindo complied for a while before losing interest.*

Aurobindo was not surprised that the censorship request originated from a member of Congress – a fellow countryman. This was further proof of the extraordinary ascendancy of "the artificial glare of English prestige," of the submissive admiration with which some Indians abandoned themselves to the spirit of a middle class modelled on English society.

The Being of Light

In Baroda, Aurobindo used a horse and carriage to move about town. One day, in a busy street, the usually placid horse became startled and reared up. Aurobindo felt the carriage about to overturn. This was when a Being of Light suddenly manifested from within.**

I sat behind the dance of Danger's hooves
In the shouting street that seemed a futurist's whim,
And suddenly felt, exceeding Nature's grooves,
In me, enveloping me the body of Him.
Above my head a mighty head was seen,
A face with the calm of immortality [...]
His hair was mingled with the sun and breeze;
The world was in His heart and He was I.[18]

---
* Not until 1950, almost sixty years later, was the series "New Lamps for Old" exhumed from the *Indu Prakash* archives, published verbatim, and its author hailed by historians as a precursor of the militant Nationalism which eventually reshaped the *Indian National Congress* into a political institution.
** The memory remained vivid enough that, forty years later, Aurobindo could relive it in this poem.

The Being of Light prevented the accident. The horse calmed down. All returned to normal. No one noticed anything in the busy street. For the second time since his arrival in India, Aurobindo had experienced a world beyond the world.

Gandhi

In this notable year 1893, Bombay witnessed the arrival of Aurobindo and, two months later, the departure of Mohandas Gandhi.

Three years older than Aurobindo, Gandhi had also studied in England for his law degree. After admission to the Bar, he returned to India in 1891 but was forced to abandon the practice of law in Bombay because of panic attacks suffered during public hearings. Resigning himself to the life of a clerk in his brother's law practice, he settled in his hometown in Gujarat. When his brother, Laximidas, was implicated in an obscure case of theft by the court of the local Maharajah, Gandhi tried to help him by petitioning the English magistrate in charge of the case. Rebuked by the magistrate, Gandhi flew into a fury, refusing to admit the impropriety of his request. "Weeping and foaming with rage,"[19] he further aggravated the situation by demanding an apology from the magistrate. For Gandhi, the incident, which stood to jeopardise his legal career, illustrated the racial arrogance of the English. Sickened to the core, he jumped at an offer from a prosperous law firm in Johannesburg, South Africa, and left India. He was not to return until twenty-two years later. Gandhi sailed from Bombay to South Africa in April 1893, exactly two months after Aurobindo's arrival in India.

On 15 August 15 1893, Aurobindo celebrated his twenty-first birthday.

JNANA – KNOWLEDGE

HIMALAYA

ASSAM

BENGAL

• Deoghar •Dacca
Khulna
Chandernagore • •Barisal
Calcutta

GUJARAT

•Baroda
•Chandod
•Surat

•Nagpur

MAHARASHTRA

•Bombay

•Pondicherry

INDIA

CHAPTER II

1894-1899

At Home in India

Family Visit

In February 1894, Aurobindo made his first trip to Bengal to meet his family. The Indian railway system was undergoing a rapid expansion. Some 30,000 miles of tracks connected almost all major cities, and crossing the country from West to East took fewer than four days. After climbing the Rajasthan Plateau and travelling onward through the fertile northern plains, the train descended toward the Ganges Valley and Calcutta. In Bihar, Aurobindo took a branch line to proceed to Deoghar, where his maternal grandfather, Rajnarayan, had retired to the dry and temperate climate south of the Himalayan Range. The presence of a well-known temple dedicated to Lord Shiva made it a favourite stopover town for pilgrims, who sometimes called in to pay their respects to Rajnarayan, the old *Brahmo Samaj** militant. The whole family gathered there for the *Puja*** season, to escape the heat of Calcutta and South Bengal. The arrival of the young traveller aroused great curiosity. As he alighted from his coach, Aurobindo was surrounded with overjoyed exclamations from a group of young girls and women, in which he felt at a loss to recognise his aunts, sister and cousin. His grandfather saved him by enveloping him in his arms. Aurobindo's sister Sarojini, five years his junior, remembered: "A delicate face and a long mane of hair cut in the English fashion." She found him very shy: "It was hard to penetrate his reserve and communicate with him."[20] Barin, his younger brother, who Aurobindo was meeting for the first time, found in his *Sejda* [elder brother] "a strange friend... at once a playmate and a guide, with a quiet and absorbed look and almost always lost in deep studies."[21] For his cousin Basanti, the most intriguing was the content of the steamer trunks, which she imagined to be packed with sumptuous costumes and rare perfumes. "What? A few ordinary clothes and books, just books! We are all here to have fun on vacation and chat pleasantly. Is Auro-dada going to spend all his time reading, and then take pleasure in it?" She was only reassured when she realised that her "Auro-dada" was quite capable of holding his place in the family circle and participating in the fun.[22]

---

*   A 19th century monotheistic reformist movement aimed at ridding Hinduism of its more controversial rituals, image worship and the caste system, and adopting some Christian practices instead.
** Ceremony of communication with a god or spirit through invocations, prayers, songs and rituals.

A man of the heart, with deep-seated convictions, a scholar and lover of the *Upanishads*, Grandfather Rajnarayan appreciated this grandson whom he knew loved poetry. The two shared the habit of bursting into laughter at the slightest provocation, and the merriment of the grandfather and grandson soon spread to all. However, perhaps because the *Brahmo Samaj* movement sought to reform certain practices of Hinduism by aligning with Western Christianity, Aurobindo never adhered to his grandfather's religious conceptions. Rajnarayan would nevertheless support his grandson's fight against the colonial regime and would always offer his love and a place to rest when needed.

Among the other adults, Aurobindo identified his Aunt Lilavati, his mother's younger sister, and her husband, Krishna Kumar Mitra. Both would play a crucial role in his life over the next fifteen years, participating in his struggle, risking their safety and offering their home in Calcutta to shelter him at vital times. A university professor and editor of a political weekly (the *Sanjivani*), Krishna Mitra was a leading critic of the regime, denouncing instances of ruthless capitalism and land devastation, notably among Bengal's indigo plantations and Assam's tea estates. Friends of Rabindranath Tagore and Vivekananda,* Lilavati and Krishna Kumar personified this class of educated Bengalis whom the British would neither seduce nor subjugate.

Another uncle whom Aurobindo learnt to appreciate was his mother's younger brother, Jogen, to whom he affectionately bestowed the distinction "Prophet of

---

* Vivekananda: main disciple of Ramakrishna, Bengal's great spiritual figure who passed away in 1886.

Isabgol" (a medicinal plant purported to soothe upset stomachs which Jogen recommended for daily use). With him, the youths climbed the Nandam Hills nearby or explored the banks of the Daroa River. Only the subject of India brought gravity to Aurobindo's voice, when he evoked "her glorious past, her present degradation and her possible deliverance." "A dream, far above my young mind," sighted Barin.

Besides Aurobindo's two elder brothers, Manmohan and Benoybhusan, both still delayed in England, two people were missing from this joyful family reunion: Krishna and Swarnalotta Ghose, Aurobindo's father and mother. Krishna Ghose had passed away a year earlier, scarcely two months before Aurobindo's return home. He who had been so anxious to secure his sons' success, who had sacrificed his paternal interests to ensure their accomplishment in England, was snatched from life before he could embrace the fruits of his labours. In a dramatic turn of events, his demise seemed to have been caused by erroneous information concerning the fate of his favourite son, Aurobindo: Doctor Ghose mistakenly believed his son to have been aboard a ship that sank off Portugal, and the shock of the news, compounded with the tensions of his personal life, broke him. That evening a neighbour found him in a state of extreme prostration, from which he never recovered. He was forty-eight.

In Khulna, Bengal, where Dr Ghose had practised medicine whilst assuming well-rewarded administrative responsibilities, he was adored by everyone. He lived in a beautiful European-style house with a large domestic staff. Unfortunately, for many years, his life had been undermined by his wife's mental health, which could swing from a frightening silence to an exuberance verging on fury. At the time Dr Ghose and Swarnalotta had accompanied their sons to England, he had left his pregnant wife in a London psychiatric clinic, which diagnosed her condition as manic-depressive psychosis. In London, Swarnalotta gave birth to Barin, their fourth son, but on her return to India, the internal bipolar storms had redoubled. The doctor finally resigned himself to parting from his wife. He found a comfortable bungalow in a village near Deoghar and left her in charge of their two youngest, Sarojini and Barin. But shortly thereafter, the first signs of ill-treatment had appeared, and the children had to be removed from their mother and reunited with the rest of their family.

Before leaving Deoghar, Aurobindo visited Rohini, the village where his mother lived. Swarnalotta did not recognise in him the seven-year-old child she had left in England. A scar on his finger convinced her that he was her son. From then on, in addition to the portion of his wages devoted to Sarojini's education, Aurobindo will contribute to Swarnalotta's monthly maintenance.

Bankim, Ramakrishna, Vivekananda

To his sister, who urged him to come back in a few months, Aurobindo replied: "It will be, I fear, quite impossible to come to you again so early as the Puja [season], though if I only could, I should start tomorrow. Neither my affairs, nor my finances will admit of it. Indeed it was a great mistake for me to go at all; for it has made Baroda quite intolerable to me."[23]

To keep the hours of office boredom at bay and to feel closer to his family, at least in thought, he set about tutoring himself in his mother tongue. And he read the novels of Bankim Chandra Chatterjee, the greatest Bengali contemporary writer, who had passed away in April 1894. Enthused after reading his works, Aurobindo decided to pay tribute to his talent by publishing a series of articles in the July-August issues of Deshpande's *Indu Prakash*. Referring to Bankim's ten novels and critical essays as "pure gold", he added: "Of his style I shall hardly trust myself to speak. To describe its beauty, terseness, strength and sweetness is too high a task for a pen like mine. I will remark this only that what marks Bankim above all, is his unfailing sense of beauty."[24]

But Bankim was not only a peerless prose stylist. His stories sought nothing less than to foster a cultural renaissance. Through Bankim's historical novels, "the desire for a nobler and more inspiring patriotism is growing more intense," declared Aurobindo. In his masterpiece, *Anandamath* [Monastery of Bliss, 1882], which narrated the struggle of a group of Sannyasins taking up arms against British tax collectors who starved the people, Bankim caught the imagination of the young, who had become weary of the current political climate. In them, Aurobindo perceived "the embryo of a new generation soon to be with us... a generation national to a fault, loving Bengal and her new glories."[25]

These words will come alive a few years hence, upon the occasion of the partition of Bengal,* when the Bengali

---
* See Chapter IV.

youth draw from *Anandamath* its cry of devotion to the motherland: *Bande Mataram* [I bow to you, O Mother], which will become the battle cry of the Nationalist movement throughout the country and the title of the opposition newspaper published by Aurobindo and his friends. *Bande Mataram* is now the national song of India.

Aurobindo was particularly sensitive to the spiritual dimension in Bankim's novels, which were inspired by the *Bhagavad Gita*.* His characters modelled their actions on Krishna's teaching to Arjuna on the Kurukshetra Battlefield: "Arise, slay thy enemies, enjoy a prosperous kingdom.... Abandon all laws of conduct and take refuge in Me alone; I will deliver you from all sin and evil."[26] Bankim's comments on the *Gita* were published eight years after his death, a posthumous tribute to he who declared: "There is no hope of progress for India, except in a reformed, regenerated, purified Hinduism."[27]

Concurring with Bankim's declaration, Aurobindo discerned that India's "liberation" was not only about freeing a territory from foreign occupation but restoring her primaeval spirit. He wrote: "We must land again on the eternal rock of ages."[28]

Another influence affecting these early years of reconnection with Bengali culture was the great Yogi Paramhansa Ramakrishna, who had died eight years earlier. Aurobindo pored over Ramakrishna's life, his thoughts and aphorisms, as well as over the works of his main disciple, Vivekananda, who had recently given his famous speech at the Parliament of the World's Religions in

---

* See Chapter IX on the *Bhagavad Gita,* the second major work of Indian wisdom along with *The Upanishads*.

Chicago (September 1893). "The first visible sign to the world that India was awake not only to survive but to conquer," thought Aurobindo. With Vivekananda, the philosophy of *The Upanishads* made a memorable entrance into the West, fascinating American and European audiences and attracting many followers.

Vivekananda – Ramakrishna – Bankim Chatterjee

In the long course of afflictions suffered by India over the centuries, Ramakrishna had incarnated the Flame rekindling the consciousness of his contemporaries. He inspired nineteenth century Bengal, which, thanks to him, preserved its identity despite the alien forces of disintegration: "There were always indications, always great forerunners, but it was when the flower of the educated youth of Calcutta bowed down at the feet of an illiterate Hindu ascetic, a self-illuminated ecstatic and 'mystic' without a single trace or touch of the alien thought or education upon him that the battle was won."[29]

Life in Baroda

Aurobindo had befriended an officer in the State's army, Madhavrao Jadhav, who shared his political views. Together with him, Deshpande and Madhavrao's older brother, Khaserao, a senior government official, a small casual circle of friends hosted lively exchanges late into the night. Khaserao owned a spacious mansion in Baroda's residential area and, after his return from Deoghar, Aurobindo often stayed in Khaserao's house and would eventually live there permanently.

One year, to everyone's surprise, Aurobindo brought back from Bengal a young Bengali writer, Dinendra Kumar Roy, whom he had hired to help improve his penmanship skills in his mother tongue. Compiled ten years later, Dinendra's *Memoirs*[30] provided a rare glimpse into Aurobindo's life in Baroda.

At their first encounter, Dinendra was surprised by his employer's unassuming figure, the cotton shawl flung over the shoulder, the long Indian dhoti, the mass of black hair and soft dreamy eyes. He appreciated the affability and composure of this "slight and unobtrusive figure," but did not fail to notice the air of gravity and the "firm set" of his lips, the mark of an "inflexible will".

Aurobindo went to bed late and began the day at his desk. Before his bath, he took the time to re-read what he had written the previous evening, then left for the office around eleven. In Khaserao's house, he led a sober and frugal existence, monitored by a pocket-watch he frequently consulted. He spent most of his free time writing and reading, motionless, eyes glued to the page, "like an ascetic rapt in contemplation." After dark, he worked by the light of a kerosene lamp, unruffled by mosquito bites. In England, he had acquired a taste for cigars which he indulged regularly. Indifferent to external conditions, he slept on a thin cotton mattress without complaining of the scorching summers or the cold winters. At most, he covered himself with a cotton blanket on colder nights.

Dinendra was struck by Aurobindo's generosity and casual attitude towards money, which he kept openly on his table. He drew from it according to his needs, including money orders to his family, which often left him penniless by the end of the quarter. To a visitor who expressed surprise at these bank-notes lying in full view, he replied with a smile: "Well, it is a proof that we are living in the midst of good and honest people!"[31]

At the palace, life in Baroda took on the rhythm of India. The Maharajah had assigned Aurobindo a delicate mission: to unravel a shameful incident of corruption tarnishing the reputation of the principality as well as disturbing the sleep of its ruler. Collecting incriminating evidence and testimonies, Aurobindo drafted a digest enabling his employer to see through the tangle of abuse perpetrated by his state officials and suggested judiciary measures to strengthen the State's credibility. His

Sayajirao Gaekwad III, Maharaja of Baroda, 1919

Highness, his sleep restored, was so impressed by these recommendations that he decided to move Aurobindo into the Prime Minister's office, right next to his own, and to increase his salary by 50 rupees. Aurobindo was now frequently summoned to write official State letters or the Maharajah's speeches, and sometimes was invited to share His Highness' table. The sovereign seemed to enjoy his company as he praised his sagacity. He may have thought of assigning him to a higher government position, but Aurobindo had made no secret of his desire to teach rather than seeking a bureaucratic advancement.

In early 1898 he obtained satisfaction. The Maharajah was persuaded to assign Aurobindo to a teaching post, perhaps at the insistence of the College Principal, who was eager to attach the new Cantabrigian to his faculty. Aurobindo was appointed acting professor of English literature, a position he would hold until 1901, before returning to administrative assignments at the request of the Maharajah. For three years, he prepared undergraduates for the Bombay University examinations and tutored older students in French.

"Sri Aravind Babu* came in exactly at 11:30, went straight to his room and began teaching, one of his students recalled. He would ask us to read seven or eight lines from the previous day; then his dictation and our writing commenced. He had no books or notes with him; everything was extempore. This procedure went on for one and a half hours."[32]

---

* Aravind, Arvind or Aravinda are older forms of transliteration from the Bengali. "Aurobindo", however, is the name he was best known by during his political years.

Indian education was no more than a drab reproduction of the British scholastic curriculum, the result of an impersonal administration rigidly fitting an exemplary model onto a subject society. Aurobindo felt that "it tended to dull and impoverish and tie up the naturally quick and brilliant and supple Indian intelligence, to teach it bad intellectual habits and spoil by narrow information and mechanical instruction its originality and productivity."[33]

To a student who asked how to improve his literary style, he replied: "Do not be anybody's slave, but be your own master. Therefore you may read any good author carefully, but should think for yourself and form your own judgement. It is likely you may differ from the views of the writer. You should think for yourself and cultivate a habit of writing and in this way you will be the master of your style."[34]

He improvised special end-of-year courses, soon also attended by students of nearby Colleges; he wrote articles in the school newspaper and moderated school debates.

To his reading list, he now added the literary works assigned to his students. He had opened accounts with booksellers in Bombay and Calcutta and received his provision of books by rail, in huge wooden crates, "which lasted from eight or ten days" until the next consignment. On his shelves, Dinendra identified "collections of all the English poets from Chaucer to Swinburne," while innumerable novels were heaped up in "the corners of the room, in cupboards and steel trunks."

After the College, he was often on call for the Maharajah's correspondence. On such occasions, an armed

Turkish horseman presented himself at his door, bearing a letter from the Maharajah's secretary: "The Maharajah would be particularly pleased if you could join him for lunch." Claiming a work overload, Aurobindo sometimes declined the invitation, and it was no small wonder to Dinendra to see "this ordinary schoolmaster regarding his own duty as more important than a visit to the Maharajah's palace, while countless noblemen cherished for months on end the vain hope of obtaining even a single interview with the Maharajah."[35]

In reality, Aurobindo pursued his personal research. A man about to engage in political struggle and to become the leader of an "extremist" party would probably work at producing a program and writing speeches to electrify supporters, but he took advantage of every moment of free time to indulge in poetry.

The *Atman* experience in Bombay and the unexplained rescue of his carriage in a Baroda street had challenged his analytical approach to the world. On two occasions, mental logic had gone off the rails while an unusual phenomenon took over the normal determinism of existence. How to explain the unerring precision of his carriage rescue on a street in Baroda or the perfect synchronicity of his cosmic breakthrough upon his arrival in Bombay?

For Aurobindo, these "miracles" had to have a source; they must have followed a process. But what *was* this different "law" which seemingly belied gravity and even causality – which could impose its silence over the din of a commercial port or alter the course of an accident? He wanted to confer some internal coherence to this different order of existence.

Through their symbolic language, *The Upanishads* had begun revealing to him an architecture of human inner reality. The wisdom of the *Vedanta** undoubtedly testified to a divine coherence in which there was place for neither ambiguity nor irrationality. But how to connect the intrinsic "logic" of this monumental Revelation with his own experiences?

He had long noticed that the concentration associated with poetic composition, the sustained exertion to commit to paper the right word, the right expression, the right turn of phrase eventually gave rise to a sensation of release and euphoria. Although an initial effort was required to raise consciousness beyond the intellect and gain access to a state of unerring intuition, the sense of liberation which resulted reminded Aurobindo of the spiritual essence of the *Atman*. It was this experience he sought through poetic creation.

All poetry is an inspiration, a thing breathed into the thinking organ from above; it is recorded in the mind, but is born in the higher principle of direct knowledge or ideal vision which surpasses mind. It is in reality a revelation.[36]

With Dinendra's help, Aurobindo endeavoured to master the rules of Bengali poetic form in order to compose an epic poem in that language. During a stay in Deoghar, Barin was astounded to see him writing page after page. Aurobindo's older brother Manmohan, who had himself evolved into a skilful, Oxford-educated poet, believed he was wasting his time. After several months of toil,

---

* Philosophy of *The Upanishads*.

Aurobindo conceded: "To be original in an acquired tongue is hardly feasible."[37] He then returned to English verse.

Toward the middle of 1899, while reading the *Mahabharata*, he came across the story of Ruru and his young wife, the Princess Priyumvada. Bitten by a snake, the Princess had died on her wedding day, but was allowed to regain her life in exchange for half of her husband's life. Inspired by the subject: "...during fourteen days of continuous writing," Aurobindo composed a thousand lines, "in the mornings only of course, for I had to attend office the rest of the day and saw friends in the evening,"[38] his body becoming for a time "the harp of the spirit"[39] (in the image of *The Upanishads*).

There is a sudden exaltation, a glow... the mind itself becomes illuminated as with a rush of light and grows like a crowded and surging thoroughfare in some brilliantly lighted city, thought treading on the heels of thought faster than the tongue can express or the hand write or the memory record them.[40]

This surrender of his mental substance and his increasing subjection to the powers of intuition above the intellect were the precursor to an inner transformation well underway.

A Program of Revolution

At the end of the day, Aurobindo and his friends gathered outside Khaserao's house to talk about the country's political situation and to comment on the latest news. They spoke of Bal Gangadhar Tilak, the man whose reputation had spread beyond the borders of his native Maharashtra (the province around Bombay), the man who defied the liberal British order and openly criticised the submissiveness of Congress, of which he was a member.

Born into a traditional Hindu family and the son of a Sanskrit scholar, Tilak had pursued scientific studies brilliantly before teaching mathematics. Soon revolted by the Western domination of his country, his political commitments led him to journalism. His popular newspaper, the *Kesari*, rapidly became the main voice of Hindu Nationalism in Maharashtra.

Bal Gangadhar Tilak

A Congress delegate from the Poona district, this charismatic man with a commanding presence had gathered around him a handful of Nationalist sympathisers, who were promptly stigmatised by Congress as "extremists". To challenge the fawning passivity of the Congress and revive the courage of his countrymen, Tilak promoted the celebration of the great Maratha hero, Shivaji*. In 1896, he was accused of having contributed to inciting the assassination of a local

---

* Shivaji (1630-1680) spearheaded the Maratha revolt against the Mogul Empire and was one of the main forces behind its collapse in the 17th century.

government official and sentenced to eighteen months imprisonment. Aurobindo and his friends followed Tilak's trial with special interest and all the more so since Deshpande was one of his defence lawyers. When Tilak was released from prison in September 1898, he became a national hero.

Another seminal event stimulated discussion: the fierce resistance of South Africa's Boer community against the British Empire. Between October 1899 and May 1902, an entire population rose up to protect its land and its independence, waging guerrilla warfare against the occupying British soldiers. It would take several months of combat, the commitment of considerable armed forces and the internment of thousands of families in the first twentieth-century concentration camps in order for England to finally subdue the Boers. Aurobindo praised their courage and bravery in a long poem composed during the conflict.[41]

Contrary to the South African situation, however, Indians enjoyed overwhelming superiority in numbers. British forces were so scattered throughout the land that they often called upon local mercenaries to maintain their supremacy. But how to transform the apparently submissive attitude of the people and gather its strength to a level comparable to the Boers's? Could two centuries of subjugation be reversed?

To take on the entrenched political *status quo* and embolden his countrymen, Aurobindo envisioned a three-pronged program: first, creating a secret revolutionary organization capable of engaging in an armed insurrection; next, establishing a country-wide propaganda drive to bring Indian society around to the ideal of independence; and finally, setting up a broad-based popular movement of passive resistance and refusal to co-operate with the British regime.[42]

This program was considered utterly unrealistic, an "almost insane chimera,"[43] by most of Aurobindo's interlocutors. They argued that a mere generation would never suffice for the Indian lamb to metamorphose into a lion. But no abstract argument could deter Aurobindo, and he continued to assess the prospects of an insurrection. Guerrilla warfare backed by a popular uprising could ultimately defeat the British army: it would be enough to procure arms shipments from foreign sources to tip the scales of firepower. Moreover, it is not unthinkable that the Indian Armed Forces, which now supported the Empire, might one day turn against their English masters.

From his trips in Bengal, Aurobindo had learned that a climate of defiance was crystallising around certain personalities. In Calcutta's educated circles, people now spoke openly of rebellion. Sarala Devi Ghosal, Rabindranath Tagore's niece, promoted the training of young men in the use of the *lathi* [bamboo cane] as a weapon. Sister Nivedita,* following the precepts of her Master, Vivekananda, advocated extreme measures against the British. She was in touch with Russian anarchists and with the Japanese Nationalist artist Okakura Kakuzo. Invited to speak in Calcutta, Kakuzo declared: "You are such an educated race. Why do you let a handful

---

* Born in 1867 in Ireland as Margaret Elizabeth Noble, an author and a teacher, she became a disciple of Vivekananda after meeting him during one of his trips to the West. The first Western woman to be received in an Indian monastic order, she supported India's liberation movement until her death in 1911.

of Englishmen tread you down? Do everything you can to achieve freedom, openly as well as secretly. Japan will assist you."[44] Present at the meeting, P. Mitra, a Bengali attorney, decided to take up Okakura's challenge by creating the first *Samiti* (cultural society), which could become a youth-recruiting and training centre. Nivedita warmly supported the idea.

In 1899, in this atmosphere of incipient revolt, Baroda saw the arrival of a young Sannyasin clad in orange: Jatin Banerjee. This disciple of Vivekananda travelled throughout India in search of personal commitment to the cause of his country. He sought to learn the art of war, but a British regulation prohibited Bengalis from enlisting in the *Raj's* army. Aurobindo asked his friend Madhavrao to help the young man enrol in Baroda's armed forces. Jatin thus learnt to handle weapons and to perfect himself in the martial arts. At the same time he received from Aurobindo his first lessons in political science.

The time seemed auspicious to start the initial phase of Aurobindo's "plan", to gather the scattered threads of Bengal's protest into a broad-based organisation extending to the entire province. Under the cover of *Samitis*, the Bengali youth had to be introduced to the idea of a future uprising against the regime, so that all young men of fighting age had a chance to prepare themselves. Covertly financed by the progressive elements among the adult population, these *Samitis* were to be set up in every Bengali town and village. Everything was to be organised from the ground up.

But Aurobindo was realistic. To change people's attitudes, to shake off the resignation of some, to dispel the illusions of the others and to restore the vast, indolent body of India to self-awareness, all would depend upon his countrymen's lucidity, upon their becoming aware of their bondage. He estimated that thirty years might be necessary to set up an effective war machine, the indispensable armed wing of a national liberation movement. What mattered was to begin.

Jatin seemed the obvious choice for this first phase of communication and coordination. In 1901, having completed his military training, he left for Calcutta, carrying with him a letter of introduction addressed by Aurobindo to Sarala Devi.

CHAPTER III

1901-1903
Engagement

Famine

Did Aurobindo sense the calamities that would befall the twentieth century? This note scribbled in 1901 seemed remarkably premonitory.

The last century of the second millennium after Christ has begun; of the twenty centuries it seems the most full of incalculable possibilities & to open the widest door on destiny. The mind of humanity feels it is conscious of a voice of a distant advancing Ocean and a sound as of the wings of a mighty archangel flying towards the world, but whether to empty the vials of the wrath of God or to declare a new gospel of peace upon earth and goodwill unto men, is as yet dark to our understanding.[45]

The death of Queen Victoria in January 1901 ended the longest reign of the British monarchy. Edward VII, her son, succeeded her. Nothing changed. Except for a few gusts of defiance limited to the educated classes of Bengal, Maharashtra and Punjab, the colonial system remained the unchallenged authority in India.

In 1899 and 1900, famine had devastated the entire central and western regions of the country (from Rajasthan to Maharashtra, an area three times the size of England) and affected an estimated sixty million people. In rural sectors directly under British control, more than one million Indians had died of starvation – the worst death rate of the century (38 per 1,000 inhabitants). In the forty years from 1870 to 1910, recent studies[46] put the number of deaths by starvation in India at thirty million.

The first reflex is to attribute these tragedies to natural causes: irregular rainfall can turn arable fields into deserts from one year to the next. But a deeper examination reveals another explanation: that of human interference with the ancestral cycle of land use.

In India (as in all Southeast Asia), it was customary to maintain flexible borders among the three major types of land: forests, pastures and cultivated fields. This flexibility was accompanied by a fluid synergy among nomadic people, forest dwellers and farmers. But one of the first tasks of the British administrators had been to survey and register the land for the purpose of tax collection. With the fallow land becoming administratively arable, nomadic communities were forced into sedentary practices, thus disrupting the pace of rural life in order to bring it in line with modern rules of land management

– but at variance with climatic irregularities. The adaptability, which, in the past, had enabled people to absorb weather extremes and survive droughts, had been replaced with a deadly straitjacket. To make matters worse, a new tax-enforcement system, inaugurated mid-century, threatened Indian farmers with confiscation of their land if property taxes were not paid on time. However, refusing to take issue with the precept of economic liberalism, the British had closed their eyes to the notorious practices of "local bankers" (*Baniya* and *Sahukars*) who loaned farmers the money to pay their taxes in drought years, then proceeded to use the new British courts to strip them of their land when they could not meet their financial commitments. The drama of this unregulated capitalism was accentuated by the new railroads, which enabled traffickers to move stocks of grain from one region to another to accommodate market demands, further depleting drought-affected areas.

Faced with this indecent speculation, offered on the altar of Adam Smith's economic dogmas, the English administrators buried their heads in the sand. Emphasising the "natural" character of the disasters, they refused any assistance to the affected populations – some officials even privately justifying this do-nothing policy by echoing Malthusian pronouncements that famines are part of a "natural regulation of the population". Still, the government did its utmost to hide the statistics of these human tragedies so the nascent Nationalist opposition would not denounce these inhumane practices. After all, was it not this government's purpose to ensure a peaceful exploitation of the country in the name of liberal efficiency?

"In these hard days, the whole country is seeking refuge at my door, I have three hundred million brothers and sisters in this country – many of them die of starvation, most of them weakened by suffering and troubles are somehow dragging on. They must be helped,"[47] Aurobindo wrote to a correspondent. He was profoundly affected by the suffering he saw around him.

His longing for change became all the more intense. Only a government in the service of the people of this country, not subject to English schemes and doctrines, could save India.

Marriage

At this time, he learnt that his teaching duties were soon to end. The Maharajah, who was travelling abroad, informed him that he wished to begin writing his memoirs for which the services of his favourite wordsmith were indispensable. Before stepping down from the College, Aurobindo was granted a leave of absence for an event he had so far kept to himself: his marriage.

He was twenty-eight. For years, his friends had urged him, as was the custom in India and as his two older brothers had already done, to begin a family whilst still in the prime of life. He undoubtedly had the desire to experience the feeling of love so often evoked in his poetry, to find his "other-half": "The wife is the Shakti of the husband; that means that the husband sees his own reflection in the wife, finds the echo of his own noble aspiration in her and thereby redoubles his force."[48]

ENGAGEMENT

As is customary, he had published a matrimonial advertisement in the Calcutta press, which earned him no fewer than fifty replies.[49] After visiting the prospective fathers-in-law, he chose his future bride from a traditional Hindu family. Her father, Bhupal Chandra Bose, was an agricultural engineer. His bride elect was fourteen years old. Her name was Mrinalini.

Aurobindo and Mrinalini, 1901

The wedding took place in late April in Calcutta, according to Hindu rites. After a short stop in Deoghar to introduce Mrinalini to her new family, the newlyweds, accompanied by Aurobindo's sister, Sarojini, travelled to

Nainital. The Maharajah, who had a summer residence in this Himalayan resort, hospitably offered them a lodge on the lake. Returning to Baroda in early July, they moved into the bungalow arranged for them. Sarojini's presence reassured the young bride and left Aurobindo free to attend to his work during the day.

At the palace, he resumed supervision of the Maharajah's official correspondence. He also began compiling material for the royal memoirs (which never reached beyond the planning stage) and took over the education of the Maharajah's children while their tutor was on leave. It was with no great enthusiasm that he fulfilled this latter task for, apart from Princess Indira (who would, later on, be in the news for defying her parental choice for her marriage), the royal children showed little interest in their studies. Aurobindo concomitantly gave private English lessons to the Maharajah himself.

At home, he spent part of the evening with his wife and sister or else resumed his conversations with his friends Madhavrao and Deshpande. But above all, night after night, he returned to his reading and solitary studies.

India's Solitary Tapasya

Eight years had passed since Aurobindo had returned to India; eight years during which he had observed the colonial machinery holding the country in bondage; eight years that he had suffered India's submissiveness to what he called "the artificial glare of English prestige" and that he had dreamed of stirring his people into revolt by setting up an army of young volunteers to train for war. His countrymen's self-denial and resignation filled him with dismay. First, there were those who, out of self-interest or cowardice, collaborated with the colonial authorities. Then there were those who were afraid and would not take a stand. Finally there were the vast majority who, conscious but distraught, resigned themselves to the political expediency of a puppet Congress and an alien government.

Aurobindo pondered. What miracle could prompt the rebirth of a sovereign people after centuries of foreign occupation, first Muslim then European? What force could awaken the three hundred million individuals living in this country, instil the flame of rebellion into them?

Yet he sensed that the world's falsified appearance and life's oppressive reality held "something else". The nameless Energy that righted his carriage in a Baroda street *could* perform the miracle the country needed. But how to connect with "it"?

His intuition told him that pursuing this Energy involved going back to the source – he must delve into India's long-forgotten past in search of the soul of this ancient humanity.

> Out of the infinite silence of the past... a few voices arise which speak for it, express it and are the very utterance and soul of those unknown generations, of that vanished and now silent humanity. These are the voices of the poets.[50]

Aurobindo immersed himself in the works of three famous poets who incarnated India's ancestral history: Valmiki, Vyasa and Kalidasa. All three dominated Indian classical literature – just as Homer, Shakespeare and Dante dominated Western literature.

Their works are pictures at once minute and grandiose of three moods of our Aryan civilisation, of which the first was predominately moral, the second predominately intellectual, the third predominately material.[51]

In his *Ramayana*, written five to eight centuries before Christ, Valmiki depicted an idealised society: Prince Rama (the virtuous heir apparent) and Ravana (who abducted Rama's wife) personified the emblematic collision between good and evil. Valmiki seized on this conflict to paint a world where the social system would exist in the service of Beauty and Good – a world distant enough to lend itself to idealisation but close enough to materialise the project of a future civilisation. After all sorts of incidents, the epic culminated in a paradigm of morality and virtue, promoting and uniting society around a "meaningful tradition" in which tales of bravery and courage contributed to mould the minds of people. Thus the *Ramayana* reflected the standards of India's early ages, the heroic character of the Hindu spirit.

The second masterpiece of ancient India after the *Ramayana*, the *Mahabharata* (25.000 stanzas in its original version), depicted a more mentally complex thought. Its author, Vyasa, the poet of action, differed from Valmiki by his realism: he did not deny the code of violence prevalent in society provided it be purified and transfigured by a commitment to action free from desire. Above the ordinary ethical conduct, Vyasa erected a higher life principle based on strength and intelligence. In the civilisation he described morality and material development were powerfully influenced by intellectual considerations. Thus, in the *Mahabharata*, it was the sovereign multifaceted mental activity of an Age that we saw unfolding.

In the *Bhagavad Gita*, which made up the heart of the *Mahabharata*, Vyasa pleaded for the establishment of the Empire of the Righteous (*Dharmarajya*), an ideal government practice based on righteousness, purity and selfless dedication for the common good. Krishna, his protagonist and supreme authority in spiritual matters, placed more emphasis on action and less on peace and tranquillity than any other Hindu philosopher. Although to attain peace in God remained the ultimate goal of existence, it must be sought *through action*.

"Not by refraining from actions can a man enjoy actionlessness nor by mere renunciation does he reach his soul's perfection; for no man in the world can even for one moment remain without doing works; everyone is forced to do works, whether he will or not, by the primal qualities born of Prakriti [Nature]."[52]

Aurobindo contrasted this ancient rule of action, as exemplified by Krishna, to India's subsequent subservience and self-denial before the oppressive colonial yoke. He speculated that already several centuries before Christ, India, rather than following the Gita's exhortations in favour of a deliberate commitment to the works of the world, had sided with passivity and indolence in her search for "liberation". He attributed this historic abdication to Buddhism:

> Before the Bhagavad Gita with its great epic commentary had time deeply to influence the national mind, the heresy of Buddhism seized hold of us. Buddhism with its exaggerated emphasis on quiescence & the quiescent virtue of self-abnegation, its unwise creation of a separate class of quiescents & illuminati, its sharp distinction between monks & laymen implying the infinite inferiority of the latter, its all too facile admission of men to the higher life and its relegation of worldly action to the lowest importance possible stands at the opposite pole from the gospel of Sri Krishna and has had the very effect he deprecates; it has been the author of confusion and the destroyer of the peoples. Under its influence half the nation moved in the direction of spiritual passivity & negation, the other by a natural reaction plunged deep into a splendid but enervating materialism. As a result our race lost three parts of its ancient heroic manhood, its grasp on the world, its magnificently ordered polity and its noble social fabric.[53]

Aurobindo then proceeded to draw a parallel between some precepts of Buddhism and Christianity: both encouraged a form of political passivity to the detriment of action. For him, only a clear, yet disinterested, commitment in public affairs, as advocated by Vyasa in the *Gita*, could advance the cause of social progress. He did not mince his words:

The Christian & Buddhistic doctrine of turning the other cheek to the smiter, is as dangerous as it is impracticable. The continual European see-saw between Christ on the one side and the flesh & the devil on the other with the longer trend towards the latter comes straight from a radically false moral distinction & the lip profession of an ideal which mankind has never been either able or willing to carry into practice. The disinterested & desireless pursuit of duty is a gospel worthy of the strongest manhood; that of the cheek turned to the smiter is a gospel for cowards & weaklings.[54]

Aurobindo could not foresee that ten years later, the Christian credo of "turning the other cheek" was to convert India; that after three decades (1915-1945) of *Ahimsa* (non-violence) advocated by Gandhi, India's ethical standards would "backslide" by twenty centuries. With a quarter of its territory lost to the carving-out of Pakistan, it was a shattered India that finally recovered its independence from the British in 1947. Today, although the massacres that accompanied India's dismemberment are covered in the dust of time, one may still wonder why the country of Krishna and the *Gita*, which advocated an explicit engagement in the battles of the world, should have accepted, under Gandhi, to neglect its own spiritual values in favour of the much younger model of Christian ethics.

After Valmiki and the *Ramayana,* after Vyasa and the *Mahabharata* (and the *Bhagavad Gita*) came Kalidasa, whose poetry reflected yet another aspect of India's soul.

His works emerged in the fourth to fifth century after Christ, when the great Emperor Chandragupta II ruled over a civilisation at its zenith – a material exuberance extolling beauty and the life of the senses where painting, architecture, music, theatre, the art of gardens and jewellery reached their peak.

Kalidasa appeared in the city of Ujjayini, the capital of the Gupta Dynasty. Of privileged birth, moving in the best circles of this brilliant city, fluent in the arts and sciences, philosophy and law, he embodied the ethos of his time. Contrary to Valmiki and Vyasa, Kalidasa's characters were not concerned with the nobility of character or the ideal of heroism, but rather reflected the vital and material civilisation to which they belonged. In their actions and words, they revealed the hedonism that drove them. A supreme poet of the emotions, Kalidasa was unrivalled in his ability to endow each form, each poetic object with a harmonious and sensual beauty.

Such was the Age of Kalidasa, when India, having exhausted the possibilities of spiritual experience through intellectual effort and rational inspiration, attempted to seek God through the senses.

In his exploration, completed in July 1902, he took stock of his journey by publishing in the Madras *Indian Review* his essay on Kalidasa, which concluded with this astonishing evolutionary perspective:

> It was the supreme misfortune of India that before she was able to complete the round of her experience and gather up the fruit of her long millenniums of search and travail by commencing a fourth and more perfect

age in which moral, intellectual and material development should be all equally harmonised and all spiritualised, the inrush of barbarians broke in finally on her endless solitary *tapasya* [rigorous discipline] of effort and beat her national life into fragments... Will she yet arise, new combine her past and continue the great dream where she left it off, shaking off on the one hand the soils and filth that have grown on her in her period of downfall and futile struggle, and reasserting on the other her peculiar individuality and national type? In doing so lies her one chance of salvation.[56]

First Samiti

Mrinalini and Sarojini, Aurobindo's young wife and sister, did not adjust to their new environment. The language, the local customs, the cooking, everything was different from Bengal. They endured their discomfort in accordance with their Hindu education, with fortitude, but in a silence that spoke volumes. Aurobindo had little time to keep company with the young women. He explained his predicament to his stepfather:

> I am afraid I shall never be good for much in the way of domestic virtues. I have tried, very ineffectively, to do some part of my duty as a son, a brother and a husband, but there is something too strong in me which forces me to subordinate everything else to it.[57]

Refusing to subject them to an unsuitable life, Aurobindo decided to take Mrinalini and Sarojini back to Bengal. In April 1902, he used his annual leave to accompany them to Calcutta, where Mrinalini went home to her parents in Assam. She remained there several months.

In Calcutta, Aurobindo visited Jatin who, with the help of the attorney P. Mitra, was organising a *Samiti* to recruit Bengali youth. The campaign was gathering momentum. Aurobindo and the two men discussed the possibilities of implementing *Samitis* throughout Bengal, and they decided to inform the youth of neighbouring areas about the movement of rebellion developing. Immediately after Aurobindo's departure, Jatin set off on a propaganda tour. In Midnapore, he notably visited young members of a group founded by Jogen, Aurobindo's uncle.

Then, once again, Aurobindo made the long journey back to Baroda.

The summer of 1902 was particularly trying. In his correspondence to Mrinalini he described the consequences of the drought devastating the Principality: "The wells are all nearly dried up; the water of the Ajwa Reservoir which supplies Baroda is very low and must be quite used up by next November; the crops in the fields are all parched and withering. This means that we shall not only have famine; but there will be no water for bathing and washing up, or even, perhaps for drinking. Besides if there is famine, it is practically sure that all the officers will be put on half-pay.... For you to come to Baroda and endure all the troubles & sufferings of such a state of things is out of the question."[58]

Overworked by the Maharajah, who regarded him as "a man of great powers, and every use should be made of his talents,"[59] he turned a deaf ear to the request for yet another end-of-year report on the "Management of the State" demanded by the British authorities.
In August, he was thirty years old.

Preparations for the Rebellion

In October Sister Nivedita visited Baroda for talks with the Maharajah. As her Master, Vivekananda, had died a few months earlier, she elected to leave her monastic order to devote herself to the revolutionary cause. She toured Western India to take the pulse of the country and to raise funds. From the Maharajah, known for his independence and (veiled) criticism of the British, she hoped to obtain some encouragement, and perhaps some support.

Sister Nivedita

Aurobindo met her at the train station. Even though this was their first encounter, they had heard of each other and knew they supported the same cause. A political friendship was born instantly between them which would last until Nivedita's death in 1911.

Her meeting with the Maharajah, who prudently refrained from displaying any opposition to the British regime, was not as gratifying and Nivedita could not hide her disappointment. She had failed to sway the one Indian ruler who might have sided with the rebellion.

A month later, Barin arrived at Khaserao's house. Now twenty-two years old he had spent four years after school wandering across Northern India: a few months with his older brothers, Manmohan in Dhaka and Benoybhusan in Cooch Behar, before a commercial venture in Patna and finally Baroda, where he turned up unannounced. Aurobindo gave him some political books to read. In the evenings, Barin attended the discussions among his brother's small circle of friends and discovered their involvement in a nationwide uprising against the British. Barin could barely contain his excitement. In December, he escorted his brother to Bombay to meet a revolutionary sympathiser, a member of the ICS who had pledged funds for sending Madhavrao to Japan to train in modern techniques of guerrilla warfare.

As happened every December, this was also the Congress convention. This session was to take place in Ahmedabad, the capital of Gujarat, and was preceded by an industrial conference where the Maharajah was to deliver the dedicatory address. Written by Aurobindo, the two-hour presentation spelled out the country's ills: its increasing poverty and its plight of endemic disease and famine – all of which contrasted with Europe's prosperity. It was in the hijacking of India's political power by the East India Company, followed by the absorption of India into the British Empire, that one had to seek the causes of these glaring inequalities, underscored the speaker. Only a social revolution, "...a great national movement in which each man will work for the nation and not for himself or for his caste,"[60] would enable India to regain her place in the world. Destined for an audience of business leaders and politicians, this remarkable balancing act closed with wishes of long life and prosperity to "His Gracious Majesty, the Emperor of India" [Edward VII].

The contrast was startling between the Maharajah's bold speech at the industrial conference and, just a week later, the fawning palaver of Congress's so-called Moderate leaders: "It is for our benefit that the British power should continue to be supreme in our land," one of them proclaimed. "We plead for the permanence of British rule in India,"[61] amplified the year's chairman. Alongside the Maharajah, Aurobindo attended for the first time the proceedings of the institution he had castigated a decade earlier in his *Indu Prakash* articles. He was there only to meet with the delegate from the Poona District: Tilak.

Once introduced, Tilak drew Aurobindo outside the conference "...and talks to him for an hour in the grounds expressing his contempt for the Reformist movement and explaining his own line of action in Maharashtra." Aurobindo emerged from this meeting with the conviction that Tilak was "the one possible leader for a revolutionary party."[62]

Aurobindo then travelled to an undisclosed location in the Bombay area, where he was formally introduced (probably by Tilak) to the five-member board of the secret society planning a country-wide revolt against British rule. Little is known about this network except that it was founded several years earlier by a Rajput noble.[63] The Maharashtra branch, headed by Tilak, included some prominent political leaders. Aurobindo was thus to become the link between the educated liberal circles in the Bombay region and the old anti-establishment tradition of Bengal.

Back in Baroda, he put down on paper a few reflections inspired by recent events. It was not so much the surface events that impressed him as what he sensed behind their existence. In both the pompous inanity of the Congress debates and the ostentation of the Bombay Industrial Conference, he saw the signs of an ebbing past:

> Behind & under cover of this failure & falling back there has been slowly & silently gathering another & vaster wave the first voices of which are now being heard, the crests of whose foam are just mounting here & there into view. Soon it will push aside or assimilate its broken forerunner, occupy the sea and ride on surging and shouting to its predestined failure or triumph.[64]

Less than three years later, a foolish political blunder by the British administration would trigger a huge wave of popular unrest which would sweep throughout India.

In February 1903, Aurobindo again left for a short trip to Calcutta. He wanted to visit Barin whom he had sent two months earlier to help Jatin recruit young men for the budding *Samiti*.

Barin's easy-going demeanour alongside Jatin's strapping build must have aroused considerable curiosity. "Brother, said Barin to a young visitor, if it makes your heart ache to see India in bondage, don't waste any time, join us, this very moment!" The young man grabbed his hand: "Right, brother! From now on I'm with you."[65] His name was Abinash Bhattacharya, and he was the first recruit. He and Barin went on to seek support among the student population while Jatin trained the new recruits. The Calcutta *Samiti* was off to a promising start.

Aurobindo was introduced to Abinash, who related this encounter in his memoirs: "With his eyes fixed on me, Aurobindo Babu gazed at me for a long time. I almost lost my balance – it seemed perhaps he was wringing out the depths of my heart? I could neither close nor avert my eyes. My chest was heaving heavily. Then he examined my forehead, pressed it a number of times, then the eyelids, later turned the eyelids to examine them. Swiftly he turned my head down and started examining it by tapping gently. Then he said, 'Your first selection is good – firm in determination, a faithful and silent worker.'"[66]

Before leaving, Aurobindo travelled to Midnapore, where Uncle Jogen was proud to present the local recruits to him. He and Barin were unexpectedly invited to a target-shooting practice in a deserted canyon nearby.

Meanwhile, Mrinalini languished at her parents' house in Assam. For the second consecutive year, drought ravaged Baroda, outbreaks of the plague had appeared and famine threatened. Aurobindo could not take her back with him. It was agreed that this time, Mrinalini would seek shelter in Deoghar, at Grandfather Rajnarayan's.

The Throne of Solomon

The Maharajah spent the summer months with his family and part of his court at his summer residence in Kashmir. He asked Aurobindo to join him. Aurobindo would live almost five months in this "earthly paradise", tasting "the charm of its mountains and rivers and the ideal life dawdling along in the midst of a supreme beauty in the slowly moving leisure of a houseboat." He composed poetry, and even "the over-industrious Maharajah, whose idea of Paradise is going through administrative papers and making others write speeches for which he gets all the credit,"[67] did not lessen the enchantment of this lakeside haven.

Aurobindo (to the right) with state functionaries of Baroda

One day, he resolved to climb the "Throne of Solomon," a rocky peak above the capital Srinagar from where one overlooked the Kashmir Valley and the majestic Himalayan crests. Alone at the top, he found himself on a terrace supporting a small seventh-century temple dedicated to the god Shiva. Legend has it that Adi Shankara, the great architect of the Advaita Vedanta, had also visited the small temple sometime in the ninth century. Gazing at the boundless panorama before him – as in Bombay at the Apollo Bunder, as with the runaway horse in the Baroda street – Aurobindo was absorbed into a world beyond this world:

All had become one strange Unnameable,
An unborn sole Reality world-nude,
Topless and fathomless, for ever still.
A Silence that was Being's only word,
The unknown beginning and the voiceless end
Abolishing all things moment-seen or heard... [68]

This excerpt from a poem composed thirty years later gives an idea of the fleeting vision he never mentioned to anyone. He had had a glimpse of the Absolute, the *Brahman*.

CHAPTER IV

1903-1906

Partition of Bengal

British Schemes

October 1903.

Accompanied by one of Jatin's recruits, a young Bengali writer and lecturer named Debavrata Bose, Aurobindo journeyed to East Bengal. At Khulna, the town where his father had practised medicine, a happy crowd welcomed the son of the doctor whose dedication was still vividly remembered. Yet whenever Debavrata raised the topic of a possible challenge to colonial rule, faces clouded over and everyone fell silent. The situation was pathetic: only a handful of Indians aspired to Independence. The whole country seemed to be covered with "a black weight of darkness,"[69] felt Aurobindo.

In the *Samitis* they visited, the young recruits did not seem to understand the stakes of their engagement: "Are these the men who will take up the fight?" wondered Aurobindo. As he travelled through India he came to realise that "a secret action or preparation by itself is not likely to be effective if there is not also a wide public movement which would create a universal patriotic fervour and popularise the idea of independence as the ideal and the aim of Indian politics."[70] The awakening must take place in the people's minds: this was the foremost battle to be waged.

But quite unexpectedly an administrative decision, whose effect no one could not have foreseen, will metamorphose the country. This is known as the Partition of Bengal.

With a territory the size of England and a population of eighty million, Bengal had always been a major headache and thorn in the side of the British. Bengal's dazzling culture had often overflowed its borders to as far afield as Malaysia, Thailand or Cambodia. Greek and Roman historians suggest that it was discovering Bengal's army with its four thousand elephants that persuaded Alexander the Great to curb his ambitions in India and return home. From the twelfth century onward, Muslim invasions and Hindu retaliations had divided Bengal's territory until it fell to the Mughal Dynasty, before it was replaced, two centuries later, by the British East India Company. After the takeover of India by Queen Victoria's government in 1857, Calcutta had become the capital of the Raj and the residence of the Viceroy.

Hindus and Muslims now lived in peace in Bengal. More concentrated in the east of the province, the Muslims considered themselves as being Bengali before being Muslim. Centuries of coexistence had eroded communal tensions, reconciled the cultures and mitigated religious singularities. But peace was threatened by scheming British administrators who, for years, had been toying with the idea of dividing the province. The new Viceroy appointed in 1899, Lord Curzon, would soon put his name on record to the most egregious decision for the British Empire in India: the Partition of Bengal.

Curzon considered that "Bengal was too large a charge for any single man."[71] In a memo, the then current Governor of Bengal had agreed, adding his own prescription: "I believe that Dhaka and Mymensingh [two Eastern districts] would give less trouble if they were under Assam."[72] At the end of 1903, Curzon decided to endorse the proposed transfer of these districts to the province of Assam, and he undertook a tour of the region. During this trip, he realised the political benefit he could derive from the plan. As H. H. Risley, his Secretary of the Interior, put it: "It would split up and thereby weaken a solid body of our opponents to our rule."[73] The "opponents" were the educated Hindu Bengalis, the most politically aware group in India, who would become a linguistic minority in West Bengal in contrast to non-Bengalis, and a numerical minority in East Bengal in contrast to Muslims.

George Curzon

Curzon belonged to that long line of British administrators who, nourished by a sense of superiority in all things, did not hesitate (when necessary) to assert themselves through violence. Before him, the Viceroy Elgin had boldly declared in 1862: "India was conquered by the sword and by the sword it shall be held."[74] Forty years later, Lord Curzon voiced British aspirations aloud: "As long as we rule India, we are the greatest power in the world. If we lose it, we shall drop straightaway to a third-rate power."[75] These men were cast in the same mould. In Curzon's case, there was a personal twist of prepossession, almost an obsession, which made him confuse the Congress with the incarnation of absolute evil, the ultimate threat to the Empire. For years, the "Moderate" Congress had shown its servility and fawning compliance toward the colonial regime, never ceasing to articulate its gratitude for receiving the blessings of British governance. Yet the Viceroy neither heard nor saw. In his eyes, the Bengali "Babus" personified Congress' worst vices: insubordination, self-indulgence, complacency. They, above all, were the target of Bengal's "restructuring."

A storm of protests engulfed Bengal as the project of partition was disclosed. In his newspaper the *Bengalee*, Surendranath Banerjee, the main Bengali leader in Congress, did not mince his words: "We object to the proposed dismemberment of Bengal and we are sure the whole country will rise as one man to protest it."[76] Even the English language press in India (*The Englishman*, *The Statesman*, *The Pioneer*), usually very cooperative with the colonial government, took exception to the plan.

At Baroda, informed by a telegram from Barin, Aurobindo recorded his first reaction in a notebook: "This measure is no mere administrative proposal but a blow straight at the heart of the nation."[77] Then he drafted an article which he sent at once to Calcutta, asking Barin to print it clandestinely and to disseminate it by hand. This anonymous pamphlet, *No Compromise*, was distributed by *Samiti* members to all major newspapers as well as to political and intellectual leaders in the city.

Even an unexpected warning from Congress' year-end session – when a surprising number of delegates expressed "opposition to a project that breaks up India's unity" – failed to arouse any apprehension among English strategists. A number of Muslims, choosing to ignore the benefits they would derive from the Partition, asked the government to reconsider its decision; such was the case of Nawab Syed Amir Hussain, for example, who felt that "the partition is neither necessary nor desirable."[78] But all this still failed to affect the determination of the men in power.

In February 1904, Curzon set off for Dhaka (East Bengal), the planned capital of the new province. There he met the Muslim leader Nawab Salimullah Khan, granted him a £100.000 loan (about fifty million pounds today), and swayed the Muslims in attendance by declaring that, "The Mohamedans of Eastern Bengal would regain a unity which they have not enjoyed since the days of the old Musalman Viceroys and Kings."[79] There was no easier way to stir Muslims than to evoke their past domination of India. With a superb nonchalance – a salient feature of the *hubris* driving these high officials – Curzon chose to ignore that reawakening of the memory of Muslim invasions and the horror that went with them was playing with fire. Convinced that their position was enough justification to rearrange coloured dots on their Ordnance

Survey maps, recombining borders and territories where people had tended to the earth for centuries, they now premeditated to open the way, through their conniving, to a long period of convulsions in Bengal.

And to awakening the Indian people.

"Build a Temple"

Meanwhile, the Minister of Education in Baroda had pleaded with the Maharajah: would His Majesty consent to lend his "Cantabrigian" to the College, where his past tenure had left such excellent memories? The Maharajah, about to embark on a lengthy European tour, acquiesced and, after a four-year break, Aurobindo resumed his teaching at Baroda College. His salary was increased to 550 rupees, and he was promoted to the post of vice-principal.

Before assuming this office, he again made the trip to Calcutta to arbitrate a dispute in the *Samiti*. It was not the first time that Jatin and Barin quarrelled, the disciplinarian outlook of one clashing with the informality of the other. On previous occasions, Barin had asked his older brother to intervene, but Aurobindo had invariably invited him to solve his problems by himself. This time, however, the conflict seemed more profound. Aurobindo tried to reconcile the young men by reminding them of the cause they shared for India's liberation – but in vain. Their egos were in control. Jatin left Calcutta while Barin followed his brother back to Baroda. The first Calcutta *Samiti* had broken up.

By late October 1904, Aurobindo and Barin were settled in Khaserao Jadhav's residence in Baroda, where Mrinalini soon joined them. This was the first time in three years that the couple was reunited. While the Maharajah packed his countless steamer trunks and gave his final instructions to his Ministers, Aurobindo prepared the College programs for the next year's curriculum. Meanwhile, in Calcutta, the Viceroy's men put the final touches to their grand Partition scheme.

A rare period of domestic serenity prevailed among the residents of the hospitable mansion, which also housed the Jadhav brothers' respective families. Without news from the political field, Barin tended the garden, wrote poetry and played the *esraj**. In the evening, the entire household convened on the cool veranda to share the news of the day, but Mrinalini did not join in the general conversation. She was so shy, reported Barin, that not once had she dared to speak to him directly since their arrival in Baroda.[80]

In December, Aurobindo took to the road again, this time to attend the annual Indian Congress meeting in Bombay. This session was chaired – an exceptional occurrence – by an Englishman, Henry Cotton, a senior official of the Indian Civil Service and faithful friend of the Ghose family. (He was the man who had introduced Aurobindo to the Maharajah.) Now, from the presidential chair, Henry Cotton declared himself in favour of Indian autonomy and against the Partition of Bengal. His courageous position would cause him serious problems with his superiors, though unfortunately have no effect upon the Congress majority which, as it did every year, voted to

---
* Indian violin.

register its obsequious reverence to the colonial authorities.

Back at Baroda College, in a quiet voice, his eyes lowered as in meditation, Aurobindo resumed his literature courses with his method of "throwing light on the subject in an all-round way which went to the roots."[81] The cases of books from Bombay and Calcutta reappeared. To his reading list were now added more Sanskrit works. In his memoirs, Barin described this familiar scene: "A table, a sofa, a few chairs, all heaped pell-mell with books and a revolving book-case groaning under their weight – all thinly covered with dust; a quiet small unassuming man buried there for hours in a trance of thought and very often writing page after page of poetry."[82] A reading program found in a notebook of the time included Goethe's *Iphigenia in Tauris;* Molière, Ernest Renan, Octave Feuillet's *Roman d'un jeune homme pauvre*; several Sanskrit plays and several *Upanishads*.

Aurobindo had translated several short *Upanishads* before turning to study the most terse, the *Isha*, which holds in eighteen verses the essence of Vedantic philosophy. Over the centuries, the *Isha Upanishad* has generated a wealth of scriptural commentaries, including the great Shankara's, which Aurobindo was impatient to confront in the original text.

Since Shankara's formulation of the Advaita Vedanta, it is an accepted truth in India that the *Upanishads* postulate the principle of illusion (*Maya*) as inseparable from material existence; the solidity of the world is but a creation of *Maya*, an optical illusion, a deception of consciousness – not absolutely unreal, but real only within the space-time continuum in which we live. Once we attain

Knowledge, we realise that this material universe and everything in it have no true existence; it is merely a shadow of the Brahman. Hence there is no fundamental reason for a man to invest himself in terrestrial life and its illusory formation. By identifying with the Self or *Atman*, man's soul merges with the immutable peace of the *Brahman*, thus escaping the involvement with the world of phenomena and its inescapable dualities and antagonisms.

However, by studying the original Sanskrit, Aurobindo was to discover that *Maya* did not signify "illusion", but stood rather for the "principle of phenomenal existence", that is to say, the power by which the world of phenomena came into being. This new interpretation reintegrated the material universe as part of the All that was the Brahman. Rather than a sterile deception of consciousness, the world about us was another mode of the Absolute. This was a fundamental break with Shankara's interpretation.

As Aurobindo put it, only this conception of Maya accounted for "both the truth of sheer transcendent Absoluteness of the *Brahman* and the palpable, imperative existence of the phenomenal Universe."[83] In its principle, his metaphysical insight bridged the chasm between God "above" and God "down here".

Thus, while still in his early thirties, Aurobindo laid the ground for a philosophical argument challenging the main dogma of Brahmanic thought. He refuted the *impersonal* fulfilment of God as the ultimate goal of existence, thus breaking with the centuries-old legacy of detachment in India. Life on earth was as much a measure of the ultimate realisation as life in the beyond.

Instead of fleeing the troubles of existence by retreating into a blank enlightenment, the Yogi accepted the earthly burden and worked to embrace and better the material world by the divine Force that drove him.

In ourselves there is a spirit, a central presence greater than the series of surface personalities which, like the supreme Divine itself, is not overborne by the fate they endure. If we find out this Divine within us, if we know ourselves as this spirit which is of one essence and being with the Divine, that is our gate of deliverance and in it we can remain ourselves even in the midst of this world's disharmonies, luminous, blissful and free.[84]

Aurobindo's long, studious periods of retirement wore out Barin's patience. Though his older brother may have been revolutionising centuries of metaphysical delusion, Barin ached for a much more earthly revolution. He had devoured Bankim Chatterjee's historical novel *Anandamath* [*The Monastery of Bliss*]: the story of Sannyasins who, during the great famine of 1770 in Bengal, had taken up arms against the occupying British. Barin yearned to follow their example and outwardly to express his worship of *Bharat Mata* [Mother India]. Impulsively, he decided to go in search of a spiritual guide and a place to build a temple, intended to be a rallying point for revolutionary monks. His prospecting took him to the Vindhya Mountains of central India, then to the headwaters of the sacred river Narmada, but finally he returned with only a severe case of jungle fever.

During some evenings at Khaserao's residence, political discussions gave way to the practice of automatic writing. Barin showed a remarkable talent as a medium in communicating with the Beyond. His pen, guided by a spirit, predicted Viceroy Curzon's imminent departure from India – before the end of his term.

Aurobindo also tried his hand at automatic writing, but he soon realized the uncertain character of this technique and its ultimate unreliability.

But during one of the sessions at Khaserao's, the spirit of Ramakrishna, who had died nineteen years earlier, suddenly manifested and conveyed this message via Barin's pen: *"Arabindo, mandir karo, mandir karo"*[86] [Aurobindo, build a temple, build a temple]. To Barin, this was the clear validation of his project of warrior-monks, and Aurobindo wrote a twenty-page pamphlet (*Bhawani Mandir*, "the Temple of the Mother") profiling a religious congregation devoted to the worship of Mother India:

> What is our mother-country? It is not a piece of earth, nor a figure of speech, nor a fiction of the mind. It is a mighty Shakti [Energy]. The Shakti we call India, Bhawani Bharati, is the living unity of the Shaktis of three hundred million people... Many of us utterly overcome by tamas, the dark and heavy demon of inertia, are saying now-a-days that it is impossible; that India is decayed, bloodless and lifeless, too weak ever to recover; that our race is doomed to extinction... We have to change our natures, and become new men with new hearts, to be born again. To be born again means nothing but to revive the Brahman within us, and that is a

spiritual process, – no effort of the body or the intellect can compass it.[87]

He warned, however, against a spirituality disconnected from life: "Adoration will be dead and ineffective unless it is transmuted into Karma [action]." His text exuded the teachings of the *Bhagavad Gita*.

In writing *Bhawani Mandir*, Aurobindo complied with Barin's intuition without being convinced by the necessity of adding yet another temple to the multitude already existing in India. Ultimately, Barin's plan "fizzled out."[88] Not a new community of monks but a new attitude was the pressing necessity. Such was the meaning of Ramakrishna's communication as he understood it: "Build the temple of the spirit *within thyself*."

From time to time, Aurobindo travelled to Chandod, forty miles away on the Narmada River, to visit his friend Deshpande, who now held the post of district officer in this pilgrimage town. In the temples Aurobindo watched the ascetics and *sadhus* performing their age-old Tantric rituals. Before his eyes, a Sannyasin, while chanting a mantra, had cured Barin of his fever by asking him to drink a glass of water he had cut with a knife.

Despite his Western education, Aurobindo did not feel inclined to the attitude of doubt and disbelief so prevalent in Europe: "Abnormal, otherwise supraphysical experiences and powers, occult or Yogic, have always seemed to me something perfectly natural and credible. Consciousness in its very nature could not be limited by the ordinary physical human-animal consciousness; it must have other ranges."[89]

Occasionally, he and Deshpande went upriver to Ganganath, the monastery of Swami Brahmananda, who was rumoured to have lived for more than two hundred years. The practice of *Raja* and *Hatha Yoga* had transformed him into "a man of magnificent physique showing no signs of old age except white beard and hair, extremely tall, robust, able to walk any number of miles a day and tiring out his younger disciples."[90] His eyes half-closed, the Swami blessed the visitors who bowed before him to receive his blessings. But his eyes were wide open as he greeted Aurobindo, who returned his gaze and felt the effect of this look as "simply electric and magnetic, bringing a great sense of peace within".[91]

Despite the many promptings from his friends, Aurobindo had not felt like engaging in any yogic discipline: "a solitary salvation leaving the world to its fate was felt as almost distasteful".[92] But he now sensed that such discipline could help him in his life's activities: "I took up [Yoga] seriously when I learnt that the same Tapasya [yogic discipline] which one does to get away from the world can be turned to action – I learnt that yoga gives power and I thought: why should I not get power and use it to liberate my country?"[93]

One of Brahmananda's disciples taught him to inhale and exhale consciously, to hold his breath and make it flow through the body. And so Aurobindo began practising *pranayama** with the same intensity he put into everything he did: "I used to practise five to six hours a day, three hours in the morning and two in the evening."

---

* Control of the breath or *prana*.

The results were not long in coming: "Formerly I used to write with difficulty. For a time the flow would increase; then again it would dry up. Now it revived with astonishing vigour and I could write both prose and poetry at tremendous speed." His health improved, his body felt stronger: "Earlier I was very thin. My skin also began to be smooth and fair and there was a peculiar new substance in the saliva." He sensed "a sort of electricity all around [him]" and noticed that whenever he sat for *pranayama*, "not a single mosquito would bite [him], though plenty of mosquitoes were humming around."[94] Most surprisingly, internal visions began arising in him: "When I first began to see inwardly (and outwardly also with the open eye), a scientific friend of mine began to talk of after-images –'these are only after-images!' I asked him whether after-images remained before the eye for two minutes at a time – he said, 'no', to his knowledge only for a few seconds; I also asked him whether one could get after-images of things not around one or even not existing upon this earth since they had other shapes, another character, other hues, contours and a very different dynamism, life-movements and values – he could not reply in the affirmative."[95]

Three Cases of Madness

Mrinalini was now 18. She could not adjust to life in Baroda. After a few months, she left again to return to her parents. In a long letter dated August 1905, Aurobindo blamed his own "madness" for the difficulties of their relationship. And he asked: "Will you try to become the mad wife to match the mad husband?"

As he declared it, he deemed himself to be afflicted with three cases of madness. His first madness was to feel that none of the talents he had received from God belonged to him. This also applied to what he earned:

> I have the right to spend only so much as is necessary for the maintenance of the family and on what is absolutely needed. Whatever remains should be returned to the Divine. Until now I have been giving only one-eighth of my money to God and have been spending the rest of it on my personal happiness. I have been pursuing the life of the animal and of the thief.

His second madness concerned his desire to have the direct experience of God:

> If the Divine is there, then there must be a way of experiencing His existence, of meeting Him; however hard be the path, I have taken a firm resolution to tread it. Hindu Dharma asserts that the path is there within one's own body, in one's mind.

His third madness related to his adoration for India:

> Whereas others regard the country as an inert piece of matter and know it as the plains, the fields, the forests, the mountains and the rivers, I know my country as the Mother, I worship her and adore her accordingly. What would a son do when a demon, sitting on his mother's breast, prepares to drink her blood? Would

he sit down content to take his meals or go on enjoying himself in the company of his wife and children, or would he rather run to the rescue of his mother?[96]

This was a moment of truth for Mrinalini. Her husband's declaration might well frighten her. Aurobindo understood and tried to alleviate her fears:

You might reply: "What could a simple woman like me do in all these great works? I have neither will power, nor intelligence, I am afraid even to think of these things." There is a simple solution for it – take refuge in the Divine, step on to the path of God-realisation. He will soon cure all your deficiencies; fear gradually leaves the person who takes refuge in the Divine. You will get that strength from your devotion to God. In the beginning, you won't have to do anything more than to devote half-an-hour every day to meditate on God. You should put before Him your strong aspiration in the form of a prayer: "May I not come in the way of my husband's life, and his ideals, and in his path to God-realisation; may I become his helper and his instrument." Will you do it? [97]

By divulging to Mrinalini his inmost aspirations, Aurobindo hoped to prompt her to embrace the inner life. But in reply to his: "Will you try to become the mad wife to match the mad husband?", she wrote in the margin of his letter: "a very sweet word!" And in reply to his: "I have been pursuing the life of the animal and of the thief", she scribbled: "admirable! admirable!" These were the superficial reactions of a very young woman who was not at all ready to follow her husband.

Boycott and Swadeshi

For more than a year, Bengali opinion had been agitated over the government's imminent Partition project. From Baroda, Aurobindo was aware of the rising tension. In one sense, the letter about the three cases of madness was addressed as much to himself as to Mrinalini: the time of open action had arrived.

On 7 July 1905, the government promulgated the decree of the dismemberment of Bengal. A new province, East Bengal, was to be created by combining Assam with the easternmost districts of Bengal, which was thus divested of a substantial proportion of its population.

The news sent a shockwave across the country. In his *Bengalee* editorial, Surendranath Banerjee predicted "A Grave National Disaster. We are on the threshold of an agitation which for its intensity and universalty will be unrivalled in the annals of this province"[98] The High Court of Calcutta described the plan as a "harmful approach". While spontaneous demonstrations erupted across Bengal, speaker after speaker urged the crowds to boycott British goods. Boycott! The word spread like wildfire. Krishna Kumar (Aurobindo's uncle) wrote in his *Sanjivani* that until the Partition decree was rescinded, "the use of articles of foreign make would be regarded as the greatest sin."[99]

On 7 August, a huge crowd assembled in Calcutta with the cry of "Boycott! Boycott!" It solemnly proclaimed that, henceforth, products of Indian origin would be used instead of English products. This initiative, known as "Swadeshi", was masterly in its simplicity, as it contributed to returning a substantial economic leverage to Indian control while dealing a severe blow to British exports. "India appears to be waking up in these days... I think Curzon has broken the British Empire,"[100] Sister Nivedita bluntly declared while encouraging students to devote themselves to the national cause.

Bengali leaders urged the boycott of Manchester fabrics and Liverpool salt. Students took to the streets, chanting slogans and extending the boycott to schools and colleges. British-made textiles were burned in public squares; in September, their sale had diminished by ninety percent. With *Samitis* beginning to appear in many towns and villages, it was naturally with the song *Bande Mataram* [I bow to you, O Mother] that the young expressed their aspiration. This rapidly became the rallying cry of those demanding economic independence and yearning for political freedom.

The 16 October, the day the Partition came into effect, was a day of mourning and general strike throughout Bengal. People fasted, bathed in the Ganges and walked barefoot in long processions, chanting *Bande Mataram*. At the initiative of the poet Rabindranath Tagore, Hindus and Muslims alike attached colourful *rakhi* threads around one another's wrists, as a sign of unity. Many Muslim leaders joined in the protest. On his arrival in the capital Dhaka, the freshly appointed governor of the new province, an obscure bureaucrat by the name of Bampfylde Fuller, was greeted by a sparse crowd chanting *Bande Mataram*.

Judging the situation to be out of control, Fuller requested and obtained the application of Emergency Powers: the new province would be ruled by decrees. Meetings and public processions were prohibited; singing "Bande Mataram" was declared seditious. Non-Bengali police tracked down students and patrolled the towns and villages applying the boycott.

On 7 November, in Barisal (a port-city in East Bengal), a violent clash was narrowly avoided. As leaflets supporting Swadeshi had been printed and distributed in the streets, Fuller, surrounded by a strong police force, arrived on the scene and denounced this distribution as seditious, even though it was perfectly legal. He demanded that the perpetrators withdraw their leaflets at once. Fearing that their arrest might trigger a riot, local Bengali leaders agreed to the governor's injunction.

The scale and suddenness of the protest were surprising from a people who, until now, had always docilely obeyed. Although boycott attempts had been launched before, they had never reached this intensity. Begun as a demand for economic independence, Swadeshi would quickly come to mean far more than the origin of the clothes people wore. As Tilak put it, "like the bodies our minds should also become Swadeshi... Swadeshi thoughts should always reign in our hearts."[101] Under the leadership of Tilak, soon joined by Aurobindo and a handful of other "extremists", Swadeshi would become the symbol of India's independence in addition to being the most effective answer against the British economic juggernaut.

Viceroy Curzon would be the first casualty of the phenomenon he had set in motion. He continued to display his abysmal incomprehension of Indian society and his narrow-minded reliance on the merits of "his" reform, but behind the facade of bravado and posturing his personal situation must have been rather more precarious. Ultimately, he used the pretext of an administrative dispute with Field Marshal Kitchener, Commander in Chief of the Indian Army, to offer his resignation, which was immediately accepted by the India Office in London. Despite the affectation, his departure bore all the stigma of political disgrace. The fruits of his misguided "labour" were dismantled in 1911, when Bengal was reunited "to facilitate its administration." Lord Curzon was replaced on 18 November 1905 by Lord Minto. Barin's stint at mediumship had been right.

Call to Passive Resistance

Twelve hundred miles away in Baroda, Aurobindo savoured the last moments of calm before the storm. His daily practice of *pranayama*, accentuated by the vegetarian diet he had adopted, nurtured his sense of lightness and purity. At the College, where he filled the post of Principal, to replace the incumbent who had gone on leave, he was engrossed in organising the end-of-year examinations. In the evenings, a visitor would often find him sitting "in a contemplative mood, calm and serene, with the gravity of a man of ripe old age."[102]

If he read less, he still wrote profusely, and his notebooks were filled with drafts of ambitious writing projects. Among them, a comment on the *Isha Upanishad* showed that he reflected on the primacy of human action liberated from the ego, which the human worker of Yoga – the *Karmayogin* – was supposed to carry out in the world.

> Whatever others may do, the Karmayogin must not remove himself from the field of action and give up work in the world... He must, therefore, be ready to live out his life and work out his work calmly and without desire, seeking only through his life and actions to get nearer to Him who is the Lord of life and Master of all actions.[103]

With his friends he organised a local association promoting Swadeshi products and, on that occasion, took the floor in support of the campaign. This was his first public partisan speech.

He was outraged by the capitulation of the Indian leaders in Barisal. "No Bengali can read the account of the interview between Mr Fuller and the Barisal leaders, without a blush of shame for himself and his nation," he wrote as an introduction to an article where he warned the government:

> Let the authorities remember this, that when a Government breaks the Law, by their very act the people are absolved from the obligation of obeying the Law.

How should the Barisal leaders have reacted to Fuller's blackmail?

Surely they should have repelled the insults with a calm and simple dignity, or if that would not serve, with a self-assertion as haughty, if less violent than the self-assertion of the unmannerly official before them, and to the demand for the withdrawal of their appeal they should have returned a plain and quiet negative. And if as a result Mr Fuller were immediately to send them to the prison, or the whipping post, or the gallows itself, what difference would that make to their duty as public men & national leaders?

Hostilities had begun. Aurobindo then went on to illustrate the approach of *passive resistance*, which would become one of the main techniques used by Gandhi and his followers against the British. It was incumbent upon Indians to respond with firmness to the foreign occupier – yet they needed to account for its strength by eluding frontal assaults.

The words *Bande Mataram* must be written – printed, would be better – on every door in Barisal. Public meetings must be held as before & if they are dispersed by the police, the people must assemble in every compound where there is room for even fifty people to stand and record an oath never to submit or crouch down before the oppressor.

Aurobindo boldly termed "new Nationalism" the protest movement that was taking the country by storm through Swadeshi. He concluded his article with a reminder of the spirit that united the people of India:

"What use to cry day and night Adoration to the Mother if we have not the courage to suffer for the Mother?"[104]

National College of Bengal

The youth were on the front lines. Defying police, pickets of students prevented the selling of British goods and proclaimed their defiance by chanting the *Bande Mataram*. In October, in an attempt to muzzle their voice, a new government directive prohibited students from attending political gatherings. A further injunction threatened principals with the revocation of government grants if their pupils were caught supporting the boycott. Undaunted, the young then called for an outright boycott of all government institutions – and the Bengali intelligentsia was exhorted to re-examine the long-cherished dream of an independent educational system. This dream came unexpectedly into existence with the help of two individuals whom Aurobindo had met a few months earlier.

The first, Charu Chandra Dutt, was born with revolution in his blood. Although he graduated from the ICS and held the office of judge in Maharashtra, this did not prevent him from mixing with Irish revolutionaries and being involved with a secret society to liberate India. He had met Aurobindo almost by accident, at the Baroda Railway Station, and the two had become fast friends.

During one of his visits to Thana, where Charu Chandra Dutt was posted, Aurobindo was introduced to the second individual, Subodh Mallik, Charu's brother-in-law and heir to a shipping fortune in Calcutta. The three men had shared their feelings about the oppressive British yoke borne by their country. When Aurobindo read out his text on *Bhawani Mandir* and outlined his ideas on the spiritual dimension he perceived behind India's liberation, the two friends were left in no doubt that this man should be supported: he embodied the light capable of guiding the struggle to independence.

On 9 November, in Calcutta, every intellectual and pedagogue in the province was invited to a huge rally in support of a new Bengali educational system. Subodh Mallik chaired the meeting. During his speech, to everyone's surprise, he pledged a commitment of one hundred thousand rupees as initial funding for the "Bengal National College", adding "the call of the Mother is clear; whether big or small, we have to respond."[105] The one condition he attached to this gift was that his friend Aurobindo be appointed as the first Principal of the forthcoming institution.

The New Party

Aurobindo was of course attracted by the educational programme made possible by Subodh Mallik's gift. He fully intended to participate in it, but this was not the main purpose of his visit to Calcutta – his first since the Partition had come into effect. "I entered into political action and continued it with one aim and one alone, to get into the mind of the people a settled will for freedom and the necessity of a struggle to achieve it."[106]

He stayed at 12 Wellington Square, the spacious and elegant mansion owned by Subodh's family. This residence was a favourite gathering place of Calcutta's liberal establishment. Rabindranath Tagore called round to read his poems in the presence of the Aga Khan, while the Maharajah of Baroda rubbed shoulders with members of Congress. It was in this unexpected setting that Aurobindo had an important encounter: Bepin Chandra Pal.

A small group of Bengali intellectuals, recently converted to a more assertive brand of Nationalism by the Swadeshi campaign, aspired to distance themselves from the conciliatory reflexes of the Bengali political class, and especially from its old "Moderate" leader, Surendranath Banerjee, the publisher of the *Bengalee*. They wanted to create a "New Party", around their leader Bepin Chandra Pal, and to carry their Nationalist agenda into the Congress arena (of which Bepin was already a member). They believed that the Congress, as a natural channel between the people and the nation, was the best potential forum for reforming the country – provided it had a different majority. Therefore, for Aurobindo as for Bepin, the primary task was "to capture the Congress and to make it an instrument for revolutionary action."[107] This would strengthen the force of the boycott and Swadeshi and compel an irreversible change of Indian society.

The Congress, however, was in the hands of the so-called Moderate party, a loose aggregation of members federated around the objective of preserving British hegemony. Aurobindo distinguished two trends among these members: the Loyalists – "who regard the rule of the British bureaucracy as a dispensation of Providence [and] preach therefore a gospel of faith in the foreigner, distrust of our countrymen"; and the actual Moderates

– "a hybrid species, emotionally Nationalist, intellectually Loyalist. It is owing to this double nature that their delusions acquire an infinite power for mischief. People listen to them because they claim to be Nationalist and because a sincere Nationalist feeling not infrequently breaks through the false Loyalist reasoning."[108]

In the person of Surendranath Banerjee, Bengal possessed the quintessential Moderate politician with consummate deceit; it was from his coterie that Bepin sought to break away so he could put his oratorical talents at the service of a new cause. Supported by Aurobindo, he and his young companions – Surendranath Haldar, Chittaranjan Das and Hemendra Prasad Ghose – would soon form the nucleus of the new Bengali Nationalist party which openly challenged the Congress' Moderate ascendancy. Aurobindo and Bepin thus began a long political collaboration and a mutual friendship and admiration that would never wane.

Under Aurobindo's influence, the gracious residence at Wellington Square, with its English furniture and polished parquet floor, hosted the first debates of the New Party members, gradually becoming the unofficial headquarters for the Nationalist opposition.

By the end of 1905, Bengali politicians began implementing in earnest the educational programme decided upon under Subodh's chairmanship. A committee of experts was convened to establish a National Council of Education to act as a custodian of the new system. This Council was to be ready to operate by early 1906.

The second preoccupation of Bengali politicians at the time was that year's annual session of Congress, due to meet in Benares under the chairmanship of a

Maharashtrian Moderate leader, G. K. Gokhale. The climate of anti-partition feelings and the gains of the Swadeshi campaign posed the gravest challenge. The annual ritual of support for the British regime was threatening to collapse. This was the first time in twenty years that Congress faced such a crisis. As the deliberations got underway, opinions diverged widely between Moderates and "Extremists" (i.e., Nationalists) on how to react to the boycott of British goods. Nationalists from Punjab and Maharashtra (including Tilak) supported the Bengali delegates in their call for extending the boycott to the entire country. Gokhale reluctantly endorsed a resolution, previously watered down, in favour of the boycott on the express condition that the Nationalists refrain from blocking a resolution welcoming the Prince of Wales on his visit to India. This extraordinary piece of bargaining exemplifies the striking unreality affecting some in the Indian political class of the time.

Aurobindo, who observed the deliberations from a distance, missed nothing of the acrimonious negotiations. What unravelled before him was the essence of the task lying ahead. To all this substance of great human principles, to all this unimpeachable mental activity, he was to attempt to apply the law of the *Karmayogin*: "to work out his work calmly and without desire, seeking only through actions to get nearer to Him who is the Lord of life and Master of all actions."

In early 1906, Aurobindo returned to Baroda to finish his term and await the arrival of the English Principal he had replaced. He planned to request a leave of absence with the secret thought of a definitive furlough.

In late January, while waiting for the authorization to leave, he wrote a tragedy in verse, *Rodogune*, based on the play of the same name by Pierre Corneille. On February 28, he posed among his students for a farewell photograph. This was probably the last time he would wear a three-piece suit. To a friend who asked why he looked so placid and serene, he replied: "My prayer is answered and I will be leaving Baroda very soon."[109]

Aurobindo with his students at the College of Baroda, 1906

PART TWO

Karma – Works

Very difficult is the way of works and their mystery. He who in action can see inaction and action in inaction, he is the understanding mind among men; he doeth all works, yet is in Yoga.

Krishna teaching Arjuna
at the Battle of Kurukshetra

CHAPTER V

1906

Bande Mataram

Yugantar, a Singular Newspaper

From one end of Bengal to the other, public opinion was inflamed by the passion of the boycott and Swadeshi. The great body of India roused from its slumber. An immense force loomed.

Aurobindo was thirty-three. In his calm, controlled manner he fully intended to participate in this opportunity to shake off British rule. Although he did not exclude any course of action, even military force, to free his country, his arguments remained predicated on the right of all peoples to self-determination.

The young were particularly responsive to his ideas and he spent long hours among the Bengali youth, expounding patiently upon the Swadeshi's political implications. Among them, Ganesh Deuskar, impressed him enormously.

Nourished by classical literature, Ganesh Deuskar had demonstrated an early talent as a writer. An essay which suggested a parallel between Mughal domination and the current colonial oppression revived the memory of Shivaji, the great Maratha conqueror in the 17th century. This essay was his first literary success and it earned him Rabindranath Tagore's encouragement.

Another essay on Britain's economic responsibility in India, backed by damning statistics, widened his readership. Although critical appraisal of the British management in India had already been put forward by Moderate Indian economists,* whose restrained diagnoses nevertheless had to concede that "the poverty of the Indian population at the present day is unparalleled in any civilised country"[1], Ganesh Deuskar's style was accessible to all. His book, *Desher Katha*, brought to light the commercial and industrial exploitation of India in blatant minutiae, just as, at the same time, it was being challenged in the streets by the Swadeshi campaign. Only after several reprints had circulated throughout Bengal would the police notice its influence among the young Swadeshi protesters and initiate prosecutions to censor the book. Finally, in 1910, it would be banned but would continue to circulate underground.

Barin epitomised another aspect of youth involvement in Bengal's rebellion. He concurred with his older brother on the need to uphold one's political position with a consistent will to action; otherwise there could only ensue a helpless floundering with the self-same impotence demonstrated by the current Congress. Rhetoric and

---
* Notably Dadabhai Naoroji and Romesh Dutt.

words alone would never dislodge the British. For Barin, the use of unequivocal force, even firearms, was therefore justified against the invaders.

Never short of ideas, he suggested the creation of a protest newspaper, "which was to preach open revolt and the absolute denial of British rule."[2] His brother supported this project, and in mid-March the *Yugantar* [*New Era*] was born. Two weeks later, Aurobindo set the tone of the new publication by writing its first Bengali editorial, "Our Political Ideal", in which he merely expressed the reality of what he saw around him. Firstly, he vehemently denied the "benefits" that British civilisation was supposed to have brought to India:

> For a nation whose mind and body are dependent on others, railways, telegraph, electricity, municipalities, universities, and National Congress – all the discoveries of science and all things belonging to Western political life – are only toys. It is only what is obtained by one's own exertion which is a right; the gift of others does not constitute a right. What Ripon* has given to-day, Curzon will take away tomorrow; at a thousand meetings and associations, we shall cry loudly saying, "Alas! Our toys are gone, what a great injustice!" Childishness is a main symptom of our present political life.

Another "benefit" brought by civilised England was servitude:

> We are slaves even if we get high posts; the Civilian, the Judge, the Municipal Commissioners, the Chairman of

---
* Former Viceroy of India preceding Lord Curzon.

the District Board, the Syndicate of the University, the Member of the Legislative Council wear chains; all of them are playing on the stage wearing chains. But then we have become so low-minded that we do not feel ashamed to boast of those chains being made of gold or silver. Slavery has like a thick fog enveloped our entire life.

Next, he attacked the distinguished Congress Assembly, which was supposed to counterbalance British ascendancy by introducing a measure of Indian influence in governing the country:

> Many people are proclaiming this in the name of the object of the National Congress: "The English officials are ruling the country well... We shall help them in the work of administration by annually informing them of the prayers of the Indians, and only by that means will British administration be faultless." But the officials do not accept this unasked-for help, but rather set it at naught by calling all this the slave's impudence and impertinence of unripe intelligence. Every year, the Congress appears uninvited before the officials with the object of helping them, and at last comes back with a load of insult on its head.

Nevertheless, a new dawn was approaching, "...the idea that this all-pervading subjugation cannot be borne any longer, that independence in education, commerce and political life must be earned by any means whatever, is being diffused all over the country."[3]

Distributed throughout Bengal, the *Yugantar* saw its readership soar. Aurobindo assumed editorial control, while Barin, assisted by prolific young writers, poured forth articles in a bold and energetic language – including "instructions" for urban guerrilla warfare. Surprisingly, the government censors would let these articles pass unnoticed for months before realising the impact of their "explosive" contents.

The Stormy Barisal Conference

Leaving Barin to deal with printing presses and foundry proofs, Aurobindo set out for Barisal to attend the Congress' provincial gathering which was to prepare this year's plenary session of Congress in Calcutta. On 12 April, escorted by his new friends Bepin Chandra Pal and Subodh Mallik, he joined grassroots militants on their way to Barisal, where, five months earlier, a confrontation on the boycott had almost turned violent.

Even before the conference began, chants of *Bande Mataram* burst forth from the thousands of people gathered to listen to their delegates. The head of the local police enjoined Surendranath Banerjee, the Bengali veteran of Congress' politics, to refrain from singing a song "prohibited by law". After consulting other provincial dignitaries, Surendranath refused to comply.

The following day, five thousand men marched in unison chanting the *Bande Mataram*. The police were ordered to break up their procession. They let the front rows of older delegates – among whom Aurobindo was marching – pass by unimpeded but struck mercilessly at the rank and file following behind. The strokes of *lathis* rained down upon the heads and limbs of the young volunteers who, despite the blows, continued chanting. Many were seriously injured. Frantically retracing their steps, the older delegates succeeded in stopping the bloodshed.

The next day, the right of assembly was again asserted by a six-thousand-strong crowd. They listened to their delegates presenting the agenda for the forthcoming Calcutta session, before dispersing a few hours later by order of the local magistrate. Aurobindo remained unshaken by the whole episode. He would have preferred to oppose the order to disperse but approved that "the right of public meeting was asserted in defiance of executive ukase."[4] He regarded this assertion of a quiet tenacity against a coercive and arbitrary ruling – a display of "passive resistance" – "to be not only justifiable but, under given circumstances, a duty."[5]

Defending this right of assembly, Aurobindo joined Bepin Chandra Pal on an extensive tour through Bengal's heartland. From town to town, Bepin's oratorical skills, his impassioned speeches on boycott, Swadeshi and passive resistance, roused the crowds. Aurobindo was struck by the atmosphere of "high exaltation and self-forgetfulness"[6] in the growing throngs of people. The "black weight of darkness" so prevalent in previous years had now almost completely disappeared.

Bepin Chandra Pal

Because he had not mastered the local dialects, Aurobindo remained in the background. When the public requested to hear him, Bepin replied: "Try to assimilate what I am telling you. When he speaks, he will speak only fire."[7] Despite his discretion during this six-week tour, Aurobindo's presence was reported by the Calcutta *Bengalee* newspaper, as well as by the British police. For the first time, his name appeared on the lists of CID spies.

National College

On 11 March 1906, the committee of experts created the previous December submitted its report to a solemn assembly of Bengali notables (teachers, lawyers and landowners) who had convened as a "National Council of Education". The aim would be to evolve an educational system independent from colonial rule. Aurobindo became one of ninety-two founding members of the Council.

Returning to Calcutta in late May, Aurobindo signed the historic Memorandum of Association establishing this National Council of Education. The second paragraph specified the purpose of the Council: "To impart and promote the imparting of education... not in opposition to, but standing apart from, the existing systems of Primary, Secondary and Collegiate education..."[8] "Not in opposition to..." was imposed by the Council's Moderate members. In this slight, and apparently insignificant equivocation appeared the sign of what would eventually distort the new institution into an Indianised auxiliary of British education.

To head the National College, the Council had validated the appointment of an "obscure school-master from a far-off province of India,"[9] whose association with the maverick Subodh Mallik stirred the rumour mill. Aurobindo was hardly surprised to learn that his authority would be limited to teaching matters. Administrative decisions were to be handed over to a "General Manager," a lawyer associated with the Congress and appointed to keep the new institution within the Moderates' sphere of influence. This control at a minor level of decision-making illustrated the prevailing strength of the Moderate establishment which stood as the benign intermediary between the British executive Branch and the Congress, and aspired to shape India on the European model.

Aurobindo's new position entailed a substantial salary reduction from 750 to 150 rupees per month which barely covered his personal expenses, not to mention the money he regularly sent to his family. His only luxury was Subodh Mallik's hospitality at Wellington Square.

On 15 August 1906 – his thirty-fourth birthday – he delivered the College's inaugural address before one hundred and fifty students and twenty professors, including Ganesh Deuskar, the author of the popular economic essay, who was enlisted to teach … Bengali.

The College curriculum included Sanskrit studies, political science, history, Arabic, vernacular Indian languages and Western philosophy. Aurobindo combined his duties as principal with lectures in English poetry and history. He guided academic deliberations and set up the topics of examinations.

Temple of Kali

Before assuming his duties at the College, Aurobindo had to return one last time to Baroda to obtain his statutory leave of absence from the Maharajah. Pending the official stamps on his request, he travelled to Chandod to visit Deshpande. Together they proceeded up the river to Ganganath, the monastery of Swami Brahmananda who had recently passed away.

The two friends then decided to head to Karnali Village. There, on the waterfront, stood a small temple dedicated to Kali, the Mother, who destroys obstacles in spiritual life. Aurobindo climbed the steps leading to the shrine and faced a carved statue of Kali, adorned with shimmering fabrics and jewellery. And... once again, Aurobindo gazed in wonderment, his consciousness captivated in an "elsewhere" outside any earthly reference. A Presence pervaded the atmosphere. He was face to face with "Her."

Eyes open, he had merged with a Reality beyond appearances, a life that had not been there a second before, a space vibrating with an energy unknown in the physical worlds. He summarised his experience at the small temple of Kali with these words: "After that, I came to believe in God."[11]

In subsequent correspondence with his disciples, he would allude to these spontaneous experiences which seemed to arise, without any apparent logic:

> One stands upon a mountain ridge and glimpses or mentally feels a wideness, a pervasiveness, a nameless Vast in Nature; then suddenly there comes the touch, a

revelation, a flooding, the mental loses itself in the spiritual, one bears the first invasion of the Infinite. Or you stand before a temple of Kali beside a sacred river and see what? – a sculpture, a gracious piece of architecture, but in a moment mysteriously, unexpectedly there is instead a Presence, a Power, a Face that looks into yours, an inner sight in you has regarded the World-Mother. [...] All things in the Lila [the Divine play] can turn into windows that open on the hidden Reality. Still so long as one is satisfied with looking through windows, the gain is only initial; one day one will have to take up the pilgrim's staff and start out to journey there where the Reality is for ever manifest and present.[12]

A Political Maelstrom

The political agitation of the Swadeshi campaign made confrontation inevitable between the Moderates – who intended India to remain within the British fold – and the "Extremists", for whom the season of "petitionary politics" had lasted far too long.

The recent appointments at the head of the British hierarchy had raised hopes. But John Morley, the new Secretary of State for India, though labelled as liberal, had promptly disappointed by declaring that the Partition of Bengal was "there to stay."[13] The second brain of this two-headed government, the new Viceroy, Minto, was well-known for his connections in the British conservative party and even more famous for his equestrian achievements at the Epsom Derby. Both had planned a package of modest reforms, including local elections in Bengal to choose representatives for *consultative* Councils.

John Morley – Viceroy Minto
G.K. Gohhale – Pherozeshah Mehta – Surendranath Banerjee

In the new province of East Bengal, the government registered a first setback when the appointed governor resigned. Scarcely ten months in office, Bampfylde Fuller ("the petty tyrant,"[14] as Aurobindo nicknamed him) had to be disavowed in his decision to punish two Bengali schools involved in the boycott. His departure was a victory for the popular forces and a blow to the regime.

In the West of the country, in Maharashtra and Bombay, a coterie led by two lawyers, Pherozeshah Mehta and

G.K. Gokhale, ruled supreme over the Congress' formal apparatus, which they had managed to keep under iron-fisted control despite vehement opposition from Tilak and his Nationalist allies.

To the east, in Bengal, Moderate opinion (still prevailing in the middle class) was incarnated by Surendranath Banerjee, the Congress veteran whose authority was now disputed by Bepin Chandra's New Party.

Facing these Anglophile monoliths, there gathered a still formless Nationalist opposition, comprised of intellectuals, students and labour leaders, backed by an immense popular aspiration, which was both the issue and the unknown in the conflict.

For the present, all eyes were on Calcutta and the appointment of the president for the forthcoming Congress. As the leader of the Moderate party in the host city, it was incumbent upon Surendranath Banerjee to find an appropriate man for the position. But this time, the task was particularly arduous. The presence of a growing number of grass-root extremists, trained by boycotts and street protests, threatened to shatter the cultish Congress consensus of past years. To avoid a total debacle, it was essential to block Tilak from gaining the presidency, which would spell a substantial, and perhaps irrevocable, advance for the extremists. "The man of action in the Presidential chair of the Congress! The Anglo-Indian envisages the idea and sees in it the very image of his doom,"[15] needled Aurobindo.

Weeks of procrastination went by. From Bombay, the Mehta-Gokhale clan threatened to change the Congress' venue if Calcutta could not find a president. The controversy spread into all the Moderate-leaning English newspapers....

This is when Bepin had an inspirational flash of brilliance. With the aim of breaking the Moderates' monopoly in the Anglo-Indian Press, he decided to set up an English-speaking opposition newspaper. The Nationalist opposition, hitherto scattered among a few Indian provinces, had been voiced only in local languages (such as Barin's Bengali *Yugantar*); in English, however, it would gain cohesion and a national audience. On 5 August 1906, Bepin communicated his idea to Aurobindo, who approved it immediately and agreed to contribute to the new journal. The next day, with five hundred rupees borrowed from a friend, Bepin registered the name of the newspaper: *Bande Mataram*.

The ink was barely dry on the first issue when Bepin had to leave Calcutta for another extensive political tour through East Bengal. Overnight, Aurobindo thus found himself responsible for publishing a national newspaper and contributing his voice to his country's struggle for freedom.

The Bande Mataram

After his work at the College, Aurobindo's second life started between the cramped printing house, which the *Bande Mataram* shared with another Nationalist Bengali paper, and Subodh Mallik's residence where he wrote his articles. In his first editorials, referring to the veritable earthquake triggered by the dismemberment of Bengal, Aurobindo delved straight into the heart of the matter:

> The issue has been fairly put between the Indian people and the alien bureaucracy. "Destroy or thou shalt be destroyed," and the issue will have to be resolved, not "it may be a century hence," but now, in the next two or three decades.[16]

In fluent language and masterly style (unassailable by the censors, but without complaisance), his articles announced the advent of a new Indian political consciousness. They prophesied the afflictions endured by India until her independence in 1947, the debacle – decades in advance – of British hegemony, and the Golgotha through which India would regain her soul.

Aurobindo plunged straight into the turbulent waters of radical politics, taking part in "washing away the walls of the political arena" and "dissolving the empty dreams" of the colonial apology in the circles of Congress.

> The true policy of the Congress movement should have been from the beginning to gather together under its flag all the elements of strength that exist in this huge country. The Brahmin Pandit and the Mahomedan Maulavi, the caste organization and the trade-union, the labourer and the artisan, the coolie at his work and the peasant in his field, none of these should have been left out of the sphere of our activities.[17]

He slammed the tireless rationale used by the Moderate leaders in order to justify their procrastination, their supposed sense of diplomacy: "The diplomacy of grown-up children! The diplomacy of the ostrich hiding its head in the sand?[18]"

His biting irony denounced a fool's game:

> The huge price India has to pay England for the inestimable privilege of being ruled by Englishmen is a small thing compared with the murderous drain by which we purchase the more exquisite privilege of being exploited by British capital.[19]

His unrelenting denunciations never resorted to complaints or lament, nor even to appeals to the foreigners' sense of justice or humanity, but uniquely to calls for faith and self-respect.

Other nations also were weak, disunited and denationalised like ourselves. It is the rallying cry of freedom that combined their scattered units drawing them together with a compelling and magical attraction.... it is only the idea of national freedom and national greatness that has that overmastering appeal.... We need faith above all things, faith in ourselves, faith in the nation, faith in India's destiny.[20]

Finally, he exhorted his countrymen to prepare to fight:

> Under certain circumstances a civil struggle becomes in reality a battle and the morality of war is different

from the morality of peace. To shrink from bloodshed and violence under such circumstances is a weakness deserving as severe a rebuke as Sri Krishna addressed to Arjuna when he shrank from the colossal civil slaughter on the field of Kurukshetra.[21]

Aurobindo's articles would soon reach far beyond Bengal; the *Bande Mataram* was the only newspaper which exposed the contradictions of colonial hegemony in the light of a resurgent, modern, democratic Nationalism, the only voice to convey India's subjugation with both scrupulous realism and an absolute faith in an emancipated and glorious national future. Aurobindo consistently brought up "Eternal India" as being at the heart of this Nationalist revival.

The new Nationalism is a creed, but it is more than a creed; it is a method, but more than a method. The new Nationalism is an attempt at a spiritual transformation of the nineteenth century Indian.[22]

The *Bande Mataram*'s spectacular success soon inflamed a barrage of hostile reactions from conventional Anglo-Indian newspapers:

If there is one pleasing feature of the present situation, it is the remarkable unanimity with which the Anglo-Indian Press has greeted our appearance in the field with a shriek of denunciation and called on Heaven and Earth and the Government and the Moderates to league together and crush us out of existence. *Statesman* and *Englishman*, *Times* and *Pioneer*, all their discordant notes meet in one concord on this grand swelling theme. The "moderate" papers of all shades, pro-Government or advocates of association with Government or advocates of association-cum-opposition, have all risen to the call. The *Hindu Patriot* rejoices at our lack of influence, the *Mirror* threatens us with the prison and the scaffold, the *Bengalee* mutters about upstart journals and warns people against the morass which is the inevitable goal, in its opinion, of a forward policy. Well, well, well! Here is an extraordinary and most inexplicable clamour about an upstart journal and a party without influence or following in the country.[23]

Two young writers, Hemendra Prasad Ghose and Shyamsundar Chakraverty, volunteered to assist Aurobindo in running and editing the newspaper. But despite Subodh's generous support, finances remained precarious.

In September 1906, a dozen companions met at Subodh's residence (by now transformed into Nationalist headquarters) to collect funds for two months' printing.

In October, the *Bande Mataram* became a public company whose shares were offered by subscriptions to its readers. Aurobindo suggested that the paper also become the official voice of Bengal's New Party. By joining with Tilak's movement in Maharashtra, this would forge a nationwide coalition, whose overarching goal would be to secure Tilak's election as the next Congress president.

In November, the newspaper moved to its own premises at 2/1 Creek Row, Calcutta, appearing in a new edition with a revamped format. All the writers, including Bepin Chandra and Aurobindo, submitted their articles anonymously and with no remuneration. The daily circulation of the *Bande Mataram* continued to be something of a miracle.

CHAPTER VI

1906-1907
Outbreak of Hostilities

Calcutta Congress

With the annual session of the Calcutta Congress now scarcely a few weeks away, the Moderate majority was determined to bar Tilak from its presidency. Calcutta's political circles were deadlocked. The suspense reached dizzying heights. Unexpectedly, a local chieftain conceived of the brilliant idea of importing a veteran Indian politician from England, Dadabhai Naoroji. Tilak and his supporters were "faced with an accomplished fact."[24]

The first Indian to sit in the British Parliament, Naoroji, former mathematics professor, was the author of a noted economics essay showing a correlation between India's impoverished condition and the British management of the economy. Though Aurobindo thought it regrettable that his essay did not "come to the inevitable conclusion that the effect could only be cured by the removal of the cause,"[25] Naoroji seemed the perfect choice for the presidential seat.

Despite this forward momentum, Aurobindo's personal participation was thrown in jeopardy as he fell ill. After several months of practising *pranayama* "...with no other result than an increased health and energy, some psycho-physical phenomena, a great outflow of poetic creation, a limited power of subtle sight mostly with the waking eye, I had a complete arrest and was at a loss."[26] The yogic progression had stopped, leaving him with the heaviness of the ordinary consciousness.

This first eclipse in the Yoga was compounded by a flu epidemic which broke out in Calcutta when the region was hit by torrential storms. Lacking the protective energy field of the *pranayama*, Aurobindo was affected and had to take to his bed. Mrinalini, who had joined him in Calcutta, nursed him as he hovered for several days between life and death. When the fever finally subsided, he left for Deoghar to recover and recharge himself.

However, there was no question of missing the session of Congress opening two weeks later. During his absence, the opposite camps clashed over the agenda of the meeting. Since the Moderates' ploy had imposed Naoroji ("the man of the past,"[28]) as the Congress president, it was imperative that the Nationalists, led by Tilak and Bepin Chandra, imposed their own agenda: boycott, Swadeshi, national education and political autonomy. The Moderates agreed to a boycott and Swadeshi, watered down and limited to Bengal, but did not want to hear about autonomy. Three days before the opening, the Nationalists gathered huge crowds in the centre of Calcutta and threatened to demand drastic amendments in the plenary session if they could not obtain an acceptable agenda. This was when Aurobindo returned from Deoghar. In political circles, it was by now an open secret that the principal of the National College was also the brilliant editor of the *Bande Mataram*. His friends swarmed around him, seeking his opinion, listening to his words.

"The Extremist Party, now with an all-India outlook, had an accession of immense strength when it was joined by Aurobindo Ghose, who proved to be a host in himself," wrote the dean of Indian historians, R.C. Majumdar, in *Struggle for Freedom,* his encompassing history of the Indian people. "Indeed the entry of this new personality in the Congress arena may be regarded as a major event of the year in Indian politics... But far more valuable to the Extremist Party than even his discourses was his own striking personality. Fired with a religious fervour he preached Nationalism as a religion, and he, the prophet of this new religion, infused, by his precepts and example, courage and strength into everyone that came in touch with him."[29]

On 26 December 1906, the 22nd Indian National Congress opened with its customary pomp and a dull, conventional presidential address. All the big names of Indian politics (Mehta, Gokhale, Tilak, Banerjee) met again in the "Subjects Committee" to discuss the terms of the resolutions that would be voted on by the full assembly. It was the first time Aurobindo took part in these secret talks. As a consummate tactician, Tilak managed to hammer out a compromise on the boycott and Swadeshi which, to the dismay of the Moderates, was endorsed by the general assembly. "You would not and could not have treated me like this in Bombay,"[30] Mehta hissed in Tilak's ear.

But it was Dadabhai Naoroji's closing speech that carried the day. Transported with joy by the agreement between Nationalists and Moderates, to everyone's surprise, the president asserted that the Congress goal was now to secure "Swaraj" (by which he meant a form of colonial autonomy). The word *Swaraj* resounded like a thunderbolt. For the first time, the Congress platform dared to mention autonomy. The next day, in the *Bande Mataram*, Aurobindo could write:

Dadabhai Naoroji

> Dadabhai Naoroji was made President in order to dish the Extremists; yet it was this Moderate President who gave us the cry of *Swaraj* which the Extremists have made their own and which is stirring the blood of the nation to great actions and great ideals.[31]

In Aurobindo's writings, in the speeches of his friends and in the heart of an entire people, *Swaraj* would soon become synonymous, not only with autonomy but with independence.

Divide and Conquer

Three months prior to the Congress session in Calcutta, on 1 October 1906, Viceroy Minto had discreetly opened his official residence at Simla to a delegation of Muslim leaders headed by the Aga Khan. The meeting, unreported at the time, was designed to set up a government strategy that has long borne the English signature of "divide and conquer." To this end, Colonel Dunlop Smith, Lord Minto's private secretary, had thoroughly prepared the meeting and even composed the draught of an address to be read to the Viceroy by the Muslim delegates, since he "knew the art of drawing up such petitions in good language."[32] The Muslim delegates would express their "worries" that the elections resulting from the forthcoming reforms in the territories would not allow the Muslim minority to be adequately represented in the provincial legislatures; therefore, they should request the application of a quota system based on religion, which alone would guarantee their fair share of power.

Everything had gone as planned. Responding to the "worries" of the seventy-odd Muslim delegates present, Minto had read a prepared statement, also carefully crafted: "You justly claim that your position should be estimated, not merely on your numerical strength but in respect to the political importance of your community and the services it has rendered to the Empire. I am entirely in accord with you... Like you, I am firmly convinced that any electoral representation in India would be doomed to mischievous failure which aimed at granting a personal enfranchisement, regardless of the belief and traditions of the communities composing the population of this continent." From the Viceroy's mouth the long dialectical career of the supranational status of Islam had begun – and it is still alive today. Historians agree that Minto's address stands as a highlight of modern sectarian politics in India.

That evening, Lady Minto copied excerpts of a letter she had just received from a government aide in her diary: "I must send your Excellency a line to say that a very, very big thing has happened today. A work of statesmanship that will affect India and Indian history for many a long year. It is nothing less than the pulling back of sixty million people [the Muslim population] from joining the rank of the seditious opposition."

Upon receiving the day's report, Secretary Morley himself expressed his enthusiasm: "All that you tell me of your Mohammedans is full of interest, and I only regret that I could not have moved unseen at your garden party."[33]

Such is the way in which these senior civil servants airily fomented discord between communities that time had begun to bind together, by summoning the grievous past of Muslim invasions and bloody strife on Indian soil.

Two days after the Calcutta Congress ended, on 30 December 1906, in the sumptuous Dhaka residence of Nawab Salimullah (the very same individual to whom Lord Curzon had lent £100000 of public money), the Muslim League was born – an organization whose stated objective was to counterbalance the influence of the Indian National Congress, considered too Hindu.

Over the next forty years, the Muslim League would develop into the principal platform for claiming separate

Muslim political treatment within India; it would be Muhammad Ali Jinnah's main political arm to launch his movement of secession from India and form a new nation, Pakistan, in 1947.

Doctrine of Passive Resistance

Aurobindo's fever lingered. He decided to leave Calcutta again with Mrinalini, handing over the *Bande Mataram* to the care of his colleagues.

In the bracing air of Deoghar, he immediately set to writing, reconnecting with the expanse of his concentration. Within a week, he composed *Prince of Edur*, a romantic drama based on the exploits of an eighth-century Rajput warrior whose motto, "Dare greatly and thou shalt be great,"[34] would not have been out of place on the *Bande Mataram* frontispiece. He felt better.

Then he wrote a new essay for the *Bande Mataram*, "The Doctrine of Passive Resistance" – and a sweeping indictment of the Indian political class. Mesmerized by the British system of government – but unaware that popular representation in Britain's Parliament had been conquered through hard-fought struggles – uninformed about other democratic systems in the world, the Indian leaders had not realized that, in the era of the steam engine and the telegraph, the ancient dialectic of entreaty had become obsolete. Perhaps worst of all, "their want of courage and faith in the nation, their rooted distrust of the national character, disbelief in Indian patriotism and blindness to the possibility of true political strength and virtue in the people, precluded them from discovering the rough and narrow way to salvation".[35]

Aurobindo's assessment of their "accomplishments" was blunt: a half-century of "political agitation" had been wasted on trivial conquests. All they had obtained turned out to be "palliatives which could not even be counted upon to palliate."[36] Incapable of objectifying their condition as vassals, blinded by the belief in English invincibility and in India's abject deficiency, they had not understood that England's "liberalism" was the result of a political calculation. London had bought their co-operation at the price of minor concessions, thus keeping the country under the yoke of colonisation at minimal cost. They had not understood that their sycophantic attitude merely vindicated Whitehall's strategists.

The singularly ineffective policy and inert nature of the Congress revealed to British statesmen – or so they thought, – the imbecility and impotence of our nation.[37]

The only strategy for India was to dare to gain freedom and independence, insisted Aurobindo.

Political freedom is the life-breath of a nation; to attempt social reform, educational reform, industrial expansion, the moral improvement of the race without aiming first and foremost at political freedom, is the very height of ignorance and futility.[38]

Contrary to Congress' "begging policy", the programme of the New Party incited to a cathartic awakening and inspired people to claim their sovereignty by urging a passive resistance (or *defensive resistance*), whose goal was to circumvent the British administration by refusing to co-operate and by boycotting foreign goods.

Aurobindo even envisioned the creation of "a central force representing either the best thought and energy of the country or else the majority of its citizens and able to enforce the views and decisions of the nation on all its constituent members."[39] From this "national authority" would flow a popular government inspired by the Indian democratic tradition of the past.

If it ever came into being, such authority would represent an insufferable threat to the central government. Hence it was in semi-clandestinity that "this popular authority will have to dispute every part of our national life and activity, one by one, step by step, with the intruding force to the extreme point of entire emancipation from alien control. This, and no less than this, is the task before us."[40]

In his sharpest political analysis, its most urgent exhortations, Aurobindo never lost sight of the fact that, confronted with violence, *passive resistance* might become tarnished with blood. This was why he warned:

> To submit to illegal or violent methods of coercion, to accept outrage and hooliganism as part of the legal procedure of the country is to be guilty of cowardice, and, by dwarfing national manhood, to sin against the divinity within ourselves and the divinity in our motherland. The moment coercion of this kind is attempted, passive resistance ceases and active resistance becomes a duty. [...] We do not want to develop a nation of women who know only how to suffer and not how to strike.[41]

This position underscored the major difference with what would be known later as Gandhi's "passive resistance". About the time when Aurobindo outlined the principles of passive resistance as part of a national struggle for emancipation, Gandhi was preparing his own protest against the discriminatory laws of the white South African regime. From the start, he actively promoted the concept of nonviolence or *ahimsa*, which excluded all forms of violence against the white supremacy. Some ten years later, when he applied it in India, the rule of nonviolence, extended to the ultimate sacrifice of one's life, would catapult Gandhi to worldwide fame. In contrast, Aurobindo continued to assert that the rule of absolute nonviolence was incompatible with the struggle for liberation.

Aurobindo's essay on passive resistance appeared in the *Bande Mataram* in seven instalments over a two-week period. In it, he detailed the methods and objectives of the Nationalist program, examined potential obstacles, and analysed the objections and concerns that the fight for independence would not fail to arouse among his countrymen. He had *seen* the resurgence of a free and strong India, and he was merely trying to expound upon the conditions for the passage.

Communal Violence

In April 1907, critical developments called Aurobindo back to Calcutta. As planned, the British had succeeded in weakening the disobedient Hindu majority. The Muslim League had formally approved the Partition of

Bengal. This was the beginning of the political fracture between India's two major communities in modern times. Communal clashes erupted in East Bengal. In March, an anti-partition rally in Comilla was attacked by a Muslim mob incited by Nawab Salimullah. The police turned a deaf ear to the Hindus' calls for help. The fighting lasted three days before the authorities intervened to restore peace. In the *Bande Mataram*, Aurobindo denounced it as a set-up:

> It is part of the policy also to attack it [the boycott and Swadeshi movement] by localities even in the affected area and not as a whole, to destroy it before the defence has organised itself; and to use as instruments the Salimullahi sect of Mahomedans, while the Police confine themselves to keeping the ring.[42]

He immediately pointed out the contradiction in seeking police help against the aggressors; to call the authorities to ensure the free exercise of the boycott and Swadeshi was tantamount to asking them to acquiesce to their own destruction. Instead, he argued, his countrymen must "look for help to the only true, political divinity, the national strength which is within ourselves".[43] He refused to consider his compatriots as "victims". India's inevitable destiny hung in the balance among adversaries who must assume their share of the conflict. This outlook – inspiring rather than comforting – stirred the Indian conformity and aroused a salutary dynamism in the ethical lethargy of the middle class.

Aurobindo read in the British exploitation of Muslim fanaticism the incapacity to face the situation by political means. For him, this way of fighting "poison with poison is a desperate and dangerous and might easily prove a fatal expedient; but with panic-stricken men the fear of the lesser danger is easily swallowed in the terror of the greater."[44] Aurobindo was alluding to the terrifying past of Muslim invasions, the massacres, looting and destruction – the suffering inflicted on India for centuries.

Yet he never stigmatised the Muslim community. The future Indian nation that he sketched out in the *Bande Mataram* columns was to be a paradigm of unity and integration:

> The new [Nationalism] overleaps every barrier; it calls to the clerk at his counter, the trader in his shop, the peasant at his plough; it summons the Brahmin from his temple and takes the hand [of] the Chandala [outcast] in his degradation; it seeks out the student in his College, the schoolboy at his books, it touches the very child in its mother's arms & the secluded zenana [harem] has thrilled to its voice; its eye searches the jungle for the Santal [indigenous tribes] and travels the hills for the wild tribes of the mountains. It cares nothing for age or sex or caste or wealth or education or respectability; it mocks at the talk of a stake in the country; it spurns aside the demand for a property qualification or a certificate of literacy. It speaks to the illiterate or the man in the street in such rude vigorous language as he best understands, to youth & the enthusiast in accents of poetry, in language of fire, to the thinker in the terms of philosophy and logic, to the Hindu it repeats the name of Kali, to the Mahomedan it spurs to action for the glory of Islam. It cries to all to

come forth, to help in God's work & remake a nation, each with what his creed or his culture, his strength, his manhood or his genius can give to the new nationality. The only qualification it asks for is a body made in the womb of an Indian mother, a heart that can feel for India, a brain that can think and plan for her greatness, a tongue that can adore her name or hands that can fight in her quarrel.[45]

Aurobindo's narrative and commentaries envisioned the "rough and narrow way to salvation". In the energy emanating from his texts, despair turned into fortitude, defeatism into faith; it was the transmutation of the lead of everyday politics into the gold of a new life to be realised.

At Subodh Mallik's, where he wrote his columns, he continued to live a simple and frugal life. Visitors could sometimes catch a glimpse of him writing on the back of an envelope while a *Bande Mataram* colleague waited nearby to finalise the next day's edition. In the evening, he might join the conversation with guests, while keeping an eye on the papers near him. Careless of his appearance, his dress, his money and his food, he spoke little and often appeared distant. Neither his slim figure nor his discreet presence impressed until one met his eyes: "wonderful, indescribable eyes,"[46] remembered a visitor. Abinash, who had left Barin's *Yugantar* to assist Aurobindo, recalled: "He was always meditating deeply about something. I found him always sitting in the same posture with a pen in his hand, deeply immersed in thought. When he looked at one, he seemed not to view one, as if mentally he was soaring far, far away."[47]

Young Revolutionary Brother

While the *Bande Mataram* grew in popularity under Aurobindo's editorship, Barin had pursued his own path of political radicalism. With the *Yugantar*, day after day he inflamed Bengal with articles bordering on the edge of sedition. The paper's success continued unabated. On the other hand, neither the collapse of the Calcutta *Samiti* nor his failure to find a temple in the jungle had weakened Barin's determination to launch a community of warrior monks.

Barin

Several months earlier Barin had planned to assassinate Bampfylde Fuller, the first governor of East Bengal, who had been installed in his capital Dhaka. With a companion, he had followed the governor's trail through the province, awaiting an opportunity to liquidate him, but a series of mishaps had frustrated his plan. Finally, informed that the governor's train would stop by a certain railway junction north of Calcutta, the accomplices had plotted to climb aboard and eliminate their man. Unfortunately, however, the train never arrived. Disappointed, they had returned to Calcutta where Aurobindo quietly listened to their story before advising them to go home.

Dejected but not defeated, Barin then returned to his idea of warrior monks. At Maniktala, on the northern outskirts of Calcutta, Dr Ghose's sons had inherited a few acres of overgrown land surrounding a dilapidated house, the *Maniktala Garden*. Even though the site did not have the prestige of the River Narmada, it was close to the city and yet distant enough to be discreet. This is where Barin decided to install his Ashram. Designed as a centre for spiritual practice and study, he would extend it into a bomb-making and training facility for revolutionary recruits. In early 1907, alternating with his journalistic activities at the *Yugantar*, Barin took possession of the Garden and began living there with a few volunteers. The discipline was strict. Beginning at four o'clock in the morning, the day included meditation and physical exercise. Upendranath lectured on the *Upanishads* and political science, Barin expounded on the *Gita* and the Russo-Japanese War, and Ullaskar drilled the recruits in the use of explosives.

CHAPTER VII

1907

Repression

The Bande Mataram *and the Virtues of the Warrior*

Amplified by Bepin's oratorical eloquence and Tilak's personal stature, the voice of the *Bande Mataram* became the people's voice. "No paper that we know of has ever evoked such a passionate personal enthusiasm as the *Bande Mataram* did during its short tenure of life,"[48] recalled a college professor. "The *Bande Mataram* gave vent to what was boiling in men's hearts. It said things that others did not, could not or dared not articulate ... somehow it touched the heart of people lulled into slavery for so long,"[49] observed another witness of the time. For Bepin, "Every morning, not only Calcutta, but the educated section of almost all parts of India looked forward to its strong statements on the burning issues of the day."[50] In their memoirs, some of Gandhi's political followers will acknowledge their debt to the *Bande Mataram's* forthright editorials. The paper's impact became known to both Gandhi in South Africa and to Nehru in England. It also contributed to the radicalization of part of the Indian community in Europe, which embraced Nationalist aims.

Finally, the *Bande Mataram* was secretly read by the British. Having gone through "The Doctrine of Passive Resistance," the director of CID, Calcutta, deemed the articles "very well written and the tone wonderfully restrained for Bengali lucubrations." He concluded that the movement "should be watched for it might develop into dangerous proportions under favourable conditions."[51] Every week, the British press, including *The Times*, reproduced excerpts from the *Bande Mataram* in its columns. Despite this free publicity, Aurobindo never addressed the English public directly, for that would be entering the realm of advocacy. His argument never drew on racial themes, accusations of tyranny or even poor British management. It was founded exclusively "on the inalienable right of a nation to independence." The position he invariably put forward was that "even if an alien rule were benevolent and beneficent, that could not be a substitute for a free and healthy national life."[52]

But when the London *Times* professed that "the Indian Nationalist movement was a pure product of racial hatred" and that "to foment hatred was the only method of these Indian agitators and the sole object of their speeches and their writings" the response of the *Bande Mataram* was lightning-swift:

> Our motives and our objects are at least as lofty and noble as those of Mazzini or of Garibaldi whose centenary the *Times* was hymning with such fervour a few

days ago. The restoration of our country to her separate existence as a nation among the nations, her exaltation to a greatness, splendour, strength, magnificence equalling and surpassing her ancient glories is the goal of our endeavours: and we have undertaken this arduous task in which we as individuals risk everything, ease, wealth, liberty, life itself it may be, not out of hatred and hostility to other nations but in the firm conviction that we are working as much in the interests of all humanity including England herself as in those of our own posterity and nation. That the struggle to realise our ideal must bring with it temporary strife, misunderstanding, hostility, disturbance, that in short, it is bound to be a struggle and not the billing and cooing of political doves, we have never attempted to deny... If England chooses to feel aggrieved by our nation-building, and obstruct it by unjust, violent or despotic means, it is she who is the aggressor and guilty of exciting hatred and ill-feeling.[53]

Aurobindo wrote his articles with the Indian middle class in mind, for "everything depended on the success or failure of the middle class in getting the people to follow it for a common salvation."[54] Aware of the damage caused by the hysterical moderate propaganda, he strove to offer reassurances:

[This movement] is not a negative current of destruction, but a positive, constructive impulse towards the making of modern India. It is not a cry of revolt and despair, but a gospel of national faith and hope. Its true description is not Extremism, but Democratic Nationalism.[55]

As he pointed out, in order to enter the spirit of this new Nationalism, the middle class needed to dispel its illusions about the approach to independence. Its first illusion was to expect India's resurgence to result miraculously and painlessly from the democratic values of the British people. Aurobindo warned:

> For a subject people, there is no royal road to emancipation. They must wade to it through struggle, sacrifice, slaughter, if necessary. History suggests no short-cut.[56]

The second illusion stemmed from the belief that ethical and religious observances might bring about the country's renaissance and deliver independence by dint of earnest moral practices. This idea (which would reach its height under Gandhi) was particularly attractive to a gentle and peaceful people, predisposed to the religious fervour, but it was yet another chimaera, and Aurobindo insisted:

> Politics is the work of the Kshatriya [warrior] and it is the virtues of the Kshatriya we must develop if we are to be morally fit for freedom.[57]

A third illusion was to expect freedom to derive from economic prosperity. For Aurobindo, progress by way of solely economic achievements was another variant of slavery. It was neither by the virtues and methods of the priest nor "by the virtues and methods of the Vaishya [merchant] that we shall finally win our independence."[58]

Repression Against the Swadeshi

New communal clashes had broken out in East Bengal. At Mymensingh, Dewangunj and Jamalpur, the same scenario repeated itself: a Swadeshi Hindu rally was attacked by a Muslim mob incited by an external leader. Although the aggression was clearly premeditated, the authorities did nothing to prevent it, and even less to protect the Hindu activists from the robbery and violence that ensued. Within a few weeks, several villages were looted, temples desecrated, women raped. Many serious injuries were reported. A few men were brutally murdered. Once order had been restored, it was the turn of the courts to step in: Swadeshi activists were usually found guilty of inciting violence while Muslim cutthroats were released. In this eastern region of Bengal, the government strategy thus worked flawlessly. While the Partition had been felt by Hindus and Muslims alike as an affront, the two communities were now divided by bitterness and anger. Still, Aurobindo refused to be fooled:

> There is no doubt considerable resentment against men like Nawab Salimullah for fomenting the disturbances; but there is no deep-seated resentment against the low-class Mahomedans who are merely the tools of men who themselves keep safely under cover. The fight

is not a fight between Hindus and Mahomedans but between the bureaucrats and Swadeshists.[59]

In the rest of the country, Swadeshi agitation had begun to spread to other provinces. In plague-prone Punjab, farmers protested against the new water rates imposed by the authorities, and riots broke out in Lahore and Rawalpindi. Sikh troops were rumoured to want to defect. A panicked provincial governor requested and obtained deportation orders for Ajit Singh, the peasant leader, and Lala Lajpat Rai, a Nationalist member of Congress. Both were imprisoned on 9 May and deported to Burma without trial. During the night, Aurobindo was awakened by a telegram informing him of their arrest. He immediately took up his pen:

Lala Lajpat Rai

Lala Lajpat Rai has been deported out of British India. The fact is its own comment.... The bureaucracy has thrown down the gauntlet. We take it up. Men of the Punjab! Race of the lion! Show these men who would stamp you into the dust that for one Lajpat they have taken away, a hundred Lajpats will arise in his place. Let them hear a hundred times louder your war-cry – *Jai Hindusthan!* [Victory to India][60]

Aurobindo knew that the time of repression had come. He even deemed logical that the government should react strongly against the Nationalists: it was proof that the threat was real, that the Swadeshi protest had reached its goal. More than ever, his own role was to expound the government's strategy, to keep public opinion aware of the regime's backroom tactics.

The British had resolved to crack down on the people involved in the Swadeshi. By unleashing mobs of Muslim thugs on Hindu protesters in Bengal, they had managed to quell dissent in several districts. However, Aurobindo anticipated that the long-term strategy against Swadeshi would rather be to attack its means of propagation: the political platform, the young and the press.

Bepin Chandra, who had undertaken an extensive lecture tour in Madras, Orissa and Andhra Pradesh, narrowly escaped Lala Lajpat Rai's fate. From London, Secretary Morley himself had to veto repeated appeals for Bepin's deportation from the governor of Madras who panicked at the sight of the huge crowds eager to hear him.

The government strategists also targeted the young. By issuing the Risley Circular, which muzzled political contestation in the educational system, the British showed they had grasped the importance of the issue: high school students were forbidden to attend political rallies, older students were prohibited from assembling and their teachers banned from discussing patriotism in classrooms.

Undaunted, Aurobindo continued to chronicle the government's crackdown. When a new decree against public gatherings was issued to complement the government's coercive arsenal, he asked, "What will be our next course? The question is whether we shall persist in carrying on our movement rigidly within the pale of the law... or follow the example of the Irish by passive resistance to the law itself."[61]

At times, however, his voice rose to a tone of commanding austerity and foreboding prophecies:

> India is going down into the valley of the shadow of death, into a great horror of darkness and suffering. Let us realise that what we are now suffering, is a small part of what we shall have to suffer, and work in that knowledge, with resolution, without hysteria. A fierce and angry spirit is spreading among the people which cries out for violent action and calls upon us to embrace death. We say, let us be prepared for death but work for life, – the life not of our perishable bodies but of our cause and country.[62]

The Trial of the Bande Mataram

On 7 June 1907, a notice was served upon the *Bande Mataram* that the Governor of Bengal was reviewing certain articles "the language of which is a direct incitement to violence and breach of the peace."[63] The threat was clear. But it took more than this to impress Aurobindo: "The question of complying or not complying with the warning does not arise. We merely note it and pass on."[64] Redoubling his condemnation of the government's duplicity against Hindu and Muslim communities, he held up to ridicule the "Comic Opera Reforms" concocted by

Secretary Morley. With biting humour, he urged his countrymen to rise to a spirit of fervent idealism:

> We cannot sufficiently admire the vigorous and unselfish efforts of the British Government to turn all India into a nation of Extremists. We had thought that it would take us long and weary years to convert all our countrymen to the Nationalist creed. Nothing of the kind. The Government of India is determined that our efforts shall not fail or take too long a time to reach fruition. It will not suffer us to preach Nationalism to the people, but in its noble haste and zeal is resolved to preserve the monopoly of the Nationalist propaganda to itself.[65]

On 1 July, police stormed the *Yugantar* premises. Enjoined to name the newspaper's editor, the young man on duty that evening brainlessly boasted that he was the head of the publication. Four days later, he was arrested, charged with sedition and imprisoned.

Panicking in his cell, he pathetically tried to retract his confession by claiming to have been abused by these "Swadeshi agitators." In an instant, the credibility of the entire movement threatened to collapse, especially as young Bhupendranath Dutt was none other than Vivekananda's own brother. Fortunately, Aurobindo could persuade him to summon his courage by suggesting a line of defence more in keeping with his ideals. At his trial, he refused to plead his innocence but read the statement Aurobindo had prepared for him: "I am solely responsible for all the articles in question. I have done what I have considered in good faith to be my duty by my country. I do not wish the prosecution to be put to the trouble and expense of proving what I have no intention to deny. I do not wish to make any other statement or to take any further action in the trial."[66]

This was the first time a political defendant challenged the competence of a British court in India. The case caused a sensation. On 24 July, Bhupendranath was sentenced to one year forced labour. He became a national hero and the *Yugantar's* prestige soared.

On 30 July, six days after Bhupendranath's sentence, a police squad descended on the cramped offices of the *Bande Mataram*. Noting that the police inspector did not have an arrest warrant, the editor on duty refused to answer his questions. After searching the premises for several hours, the police squad left with its paper harvest. Inspectors would spend two weeks sifting through their catch in the hope of establishing Aurobindo's editorial responsibility. Despite the lack of hard evidence, an arrest warrant was issued against him.

On 16 August, at dinner time, Aurobindo learnt that a police officer had showed up at the *Bande Mataram* offices with an arrest warrant. In consultation with his lawyer friends, he decided to give himself up. At the police station, he was formally charged and released on bail. The next day, the Calcutta commissioner of police served him notice to appear before the chief presidency magistrate, Judge Kingsford, on 26 August.

In Calcutta, the news of his indictment spread like wildfire. All newspapers, including those which had not spared their criticism against the *Bande Mataram*, vied with each other in testifying to Aurobindo's lack of personal ambition and patriotic feelings. The *Indian Patriot* was the most lavish in its praise: "Mr Aurobindo Ghose is no notoriety hunter, is no demagogue who wants to become prominent by courting conviction for sedition. A man of very fine culture, his is a loveable nature; merry, sparkling with wit and humour, he is one of those men to be in whose company is a joy and behind whose exterior is a steadily glowing fire of unseen devotion to a cause."[67]

But no one expressed Bengal's emotion better than the poet Rabindranath Tagore:

> *Rabindranath, O Aurobindo, bows to thee!*
> *O friend, my country's friend, O voice incarnate, free,*
> *Of India's soul!...*
> *When I behold thy face, 'mid bondage, pain and wrong*
> *And black indignities, I hear the soul's great song...*[68]

Before standing trial, Aurobindo resigned from the National College, delivering a short farewell address to the students:

> In the meeting you held yesterday I see that you expressed sympathy with me in what you call my present troubles. I don't know whether I should call them troubles at all, for the experience that I am going to undergo was long foreseen as inevitable in the discharge of the mission that I have taken up from my childhood, and I am approaching it without regret...[69]

As the trial opened on 26 August, the prosecutor had to demonstrate the seditious nature of the *Bande Mataram* articles as well as prove that Aurobindo was, in reality, its editor-in-chief. He was in the very same quandary as the Calcutta *Statesman* thundering against the *Bande Mataram's* articles: "... too diabolically clever, crammed full of sedition between the lines, but legally unattackable because of the skill of the language."[70]

Confronted with this challenge, and to make his case credible, the prosecutor fell back upon the English reprint of two subversive pieces already published in the *Yugantar*. In the absence of physical proof, however, he found it impossible to associate Aurobindo with the articles in question.

Rather than conceding defeat, the prosecutor then called in the *Bande Mataram* founder and original editor, Bepin Chandra Pal. But Bepin refused to testify against Aurobindo. Held in contempt of court, he was convicted by summary trial and sentenced to six months in jail.

The prosecutor could only give vent to his frustration: "I do not care whether Aurobindo is the editor or not. I submit that he is the newspaper itself!"

For reprinting the two *Yugantar* articles, the *Bande Mataram* was condemned in the person of its printer, a front man who had knowingly accepted this role. Judge Kingsford refuted any seditious character in the general tone of the newspaper. In acquitting Aurobindo, he noted that this is "a man of exceptionally good attainments who had differentiated himself from the ordinary staff by refusing to take any fixed salary for his labour."[71]

The news of Aurobindo's acquittal was celebrated throughout the country. Rabindranath Tagore was one of the first to congratulate him, adding in jest, "What! How you have deceived me!" Smiling, Aurobindo replied: "Not for long."

CHAPTER VIII

1907-1908

The Breakup

Head of the Nationalist Movement

The *Bande Mataram* Trial propelled Aurobindo to centre stage. "I was never ardent about fame... it was the confounded British Government that spoiled my game by prosecuting me and forcing me to be publicly known as a 'leader'."[72]

In the absence of Bepin Chandra, who was serving his sentence ("the maximum penalty permitted by the law for the crime of possessing a conscience"[73]), he became the leader of the Nationalists in Bengal. It was time to prepare his camp to attend the forthcoming session of the Congress, where the Moderates, who had lost ground in Calcutta, would seek to regain the advantage.

This time, on paper at least, the balance was on the Nationalist side. Tilak had every chance of being elected president. His party had a majority in Nagpur, where this next Congress was to convene. Sensing danger, the

Nagpur Moderates called their Bombay supreme leaders to the rescue. Pherozeshah Mehta (head of the Congress in Bombay) convened the Central Executive Committee in the presence of the British Commissioner of Police and decided there and then to move the Congress from Nagpur to Surat, where the Moderates still held a majority. In the *Bande Mataram*, Aurobindo protested vehemently:

> ...if you will not allow us a place in the assembly you call National, we will make one for ourselves out of it and around it, until one day you will find us knocking at your doors with the nation at our back and in the name of an authority even you will not dare to deny.[74]

At the beginning of December, as a preview of what was to follow at Surat, a provincial conference was convened at Midnapore [East Bengal], where Aurobindo headed the Nationalist delegates. By a narrow margin, the Moderates had elected the president of their choice. But when the Nationalists demanded that the president address the question of *Swaraj* [autonomy] without delay, he refused and continued delivering his lame acceptance speech. He was vehemently interrupted and the meeting erupted in chaos. As the president turned to Aurobindo and begged him to restore calm, Aurobindo remained impassive. The Moderates were forced to cancel the debate and move to another venue.

This was unprecedented: the Moderate machine had lost its ability to keep control over an ebullient youth who proclaimed their existence and their rejection of political stratagems. The modest provincial conference in Midnapore marked a turning point. "The Nationalist organisation is now an accomplished fact... Midnapore has taken the initiative in giving Nationalism an organised shape and form,"[75] predicted Aurobindo in the *Bande Mataram*.

In Calcutta, the name of the man who had emerged victorious from a confrontation with British justice was on everyone's lips. Somehow, people knew that he was the mastermind behind the crusade capable of freeing the country from the foreign yoke. Visitors lined up at Subodh Mallik's to meet him. On December 15, he spoke in public and outlined the Nationalist agenda.

The Manchester Guardian requested an interview. The journalist described Aurobindo as: "Grave with intensity, careless of fate or opinion, and one of the most silent men I have ever known, he was of the stuff that dreamers are made of, but dreamers who will act their dreams, indifferent to the means."[76]

Before travelling to Surat, where a decisive confrontation with the power of Indian conservatism awaited him, Aurobindo confided to Mrinalini: "At present I have not got a moment to spare; the burden of writing is on me, the burden of works regarding the Congress is on me, and also that of settling the affairs of *Bande Mataram*. I can hardly cope with the work. Besides I have my own work [Yoga] to do which I cannot neglect ... the pressure from all sides is enough to drive one mad." He pleaded with his wife to cease complaining about the material circumstances of her life in Deoghar: "If you too get restless now, it would only add to my anxiety and worry; a letter of encouragement and comfort from you would give me much strength, and I could overcome all fears and dangers with a cheerful heart."[77]

The Surat Congress: The Breakup

On the morning of 21 December 1907, a special train packed with Bengali delegates, set out for Surat. On board were all the editors of the *Bande Mataram* along with an army of young Nationalist volunteers, Aurobindo and his brother, Barin. The convoy took longer than expected to reach its destination because of the many stops caused by crowds eager to discover the face of their new hero. At each stop, men shouting "Bande Mataram" searched first-class cars, then second, finally to locate their man in a third-class compartment, a broad smile on his face. Occasionally, Aurobindo stepped down onto the tracks to say a few words, and invariably he was wreathed with garlands before the train left again. The secretary of the Moderate party (who travelled first class) tried unsuccessfully to draw Aurobindo beside him. At Bombay, a large welcome meeting had been organised. In the human wave converging onto the square to greet Aurobindo, Barin saw "the awakening of the whole nation from its age-long sleep and inertia into conscious life".[78]

Finally, on 24 December, they reached Surat. An air of festivity presided over the surroundings of the *pandal* [central pavilion]. Swarms of servants hastened around the luxurious tents sheltering the Moderate dignitaries, while the Nationalists crowded into houses, dormitories and makeshift shelters in the city centre. Tilak and Aurobindo finalised their party strategy without paying too much attention to the stream of admirers who filled the house in the hope of seeing them together.

The last Nationalist conference before the breakup of the Congress in Surat (December 1907). Aurobindo (sitting) presides while Tilak addresses the delegates.

The final delegate count stood at 1,100 for the Nationalists, against 1,300 for the Moderates. But rumours circulated that the Moderates would take advantage of their narrow majority to modify the Congress constitution so as to prevent an extremist takeover in the years to come. The young Nationalists were determined to fight back: if they could not impose themselves by the numbers, they would break up the Congress.

Someone informed Tilak that, on Gokhale's orders and in disregard of basic rules, the draft resolutions on which the Congress was to vote would not be available before the plenary session. This suggested that the Moderates were planning to renege on the positions conceded at the previous Congress session in Calcutta.

On this first day and the next, the Nationalists repeatedly tried to enter into a dialogue with the Moderates, notably concerning the question of the Congress presidency, which should be handed, if not to Tilak, then at least to Lala Lajpat Rai (just released from Burma after six months in jail). Armed with their majority, the Moderate leaders haughtily rejected all attempts at discussion.

On the afternoon of the second day, 10,000 people crowded into the *pandal* to inaugurate the 23rd plenary session of the Congress. The Moderates ran the show as if the opposite side did not exist. As several Moderate officials ascended the rostrum to endorse the new preselected Moderate president, Tilak finally received a copy of the draft resolutions. As he feared, all the Calcutta political advances had been cancelled or weakened. When Surendranath Banerjee, the Bengal Moderate leader, moved to the rostrum to add his voice to the chorus of sponsorships, loud cries arose from the Nationalist ranks. "Remember Midnapore! Remember Nagpur!" Thousands of youths screamed furiously. The session was suspended.

The power of "direct democracy", so dreaded by professional politicians, had defied the Congress "system" with its secret conclaves and fabricated majorities. The balance of forces had tipped.

The next day was decisive. The young Nationalists had informed Aurobindo of their intention to break up the Congress if they could not obtain a fair hearing. However, they would wait for his signal before throwing down the gauntlet.

At 1 pm, the *pandal* was overflowing and Aurobindo was sitting in the front row, surrounded by a dozen young Bengalis. Tilak had sent word to the officials that he desired to address the assembly before the inaugural speech of the designated president, Moderate Rash Behari Ghose, but as he approached the rostrum, the president, pretending to ignore him, launched into his speech. Facing the crowd, his arms broadly upon his chest, Tilak demanded to be heard and confronted the henchmen rushing up to restrain him. The young Nationalists rose as one. A red shoe with metal tip took flight, ricocheted on a Moderate dignitary and hit Pherozeshah Mehta. The assembly was thrown into chaos. Moderate leaders fled precipitately. Aurobindo was escorted out of the compound. The session of Surat was suspended *sine die*.

As Aurobindo would later confirm, it was he who gave the signal for the breakup. Tilak was unaware of the plan, as he felt that contesting the Moderate's practices would be enough to tip the balance of power. As Aurobindo put it, "[Tilak] will take willingly half a loaf rather than no bread, though always with a full intention of getting the whole loaf in good time".[79]

In contrast to Tilak's approach, Aurobindo saw in the dramatic breakup an opportunity to electrify the country, to free pent-up energy and bolster the desire for independence. Historical evidence suggests that the British government had envisioned the Congress breakup and was preparing for a merciless repression of the Nationalists.

In the meantime, Moderate leaders busily broadcast their version of the rupture. Then, under police escort, they improvised a rally to replace the Congress with a "Convention". Henceforth, each delegate to this new, tailor-made version of Congress would have to sign a "credo" or declaration of allegiance to the principles of Bristish-inspired liberalism. Aurobindo and the young Nationalists refused to sign; Tilak hesitated but eventually came around and agreed with his friends.

Now the Nationalist Party was a separate political entity. The new Moderates' Convention would not endure the test of time, its membership dwindling year after year. Aurobindo had been right: the Nationalist sentiment would gradually prevail as the dominant political force – despite the repression of its militants, or perhaps because of it.

Eight years later, in 1916, returning to his country after a long ordeal of deportation in Burma, Tilak would rejoin Congress and work to make it the sanctuary of a Nationalism devoted to India's complete independence. For the occasion, the Moderate party was renamed "Liberal" and committed to the goal of independence.

The three days in Surat, which mark a dramatic progress in India's political emancipation, are rarely mentioned in history books. Aurobindo's role is ignored.

Nirvana

Early in the morning on 1 January 1908, the train bringing Aurobindo and Barin back from Surat entered Baroda station.

A joyful group of friends, students who had come to greet their former professor and many unknown well-wishers awaited Aurobindo as he stepped out of his compartment. The young men clutched the carriage transporting the two brothers and escorted them to the residence of Khaserao Jadhav.

A visitor, Vishnu Bhaskar Lele, a Yogi whom Barin had met while searching for a master to chaperone his project of warrior monks, awaited them. Lele was a simple civil servant, but his eyes glowed with the evidence of an inner life.

Aurobindo disclosed to him his experiences with pranayama and the results that ensued... until the yogic progression had stopped and he could go no further. Lele listened intently and suggested that Aurobindo suspend his outer activities and join him for a meditation.

Aurobindo accepted, but not before reporting on the Surat events to the crowd of well-wishers camping on the lawns outside Khaserao's house. After answering their many eager questions, he took the time to make a courtesy call to his former employer, the Maharajah.

Finally, he joined Lele in a friend's townhouse and there, in a small room at the top, the two men sat facing each other on the floor.

> "Sit in meditation," he said, "but do not think, look only at your mind; you will see thoughts coming into it; before they can enter throw them away from you till your mind is capable of entire silence." I had never heard before of thoughts coming visibly into the mind from outside, but I did not think of either questioning the truth or the possibility, I simply sat down and did it. In a moment my mind became silent as a windless air on a high mountain summit and then I saw a thought and then another thought coming in a concrete way from outside; I flung them away before they

could enter and take hold of the brain and in three days I was free.[80]

The young people combing the city in search of Aurobindo could not possibly suspect where their hero was hiding. The silence in this room was dense, the peace compact, flawless; two human beings were suspended in a buoyant weightlessness, a suspension of existence, a vacuum, a Nothing. By wresting Aurobindo from the usual mental practice, these three days of meditation with Lele would precipitate a radical change of consciousness in Aurobindo. Now that he perceived thoughts as coming from *outside*, he controlled his mind:

> From that moment, in principle, the mental being in me became a free Intelligence, a universal Mind, not limited to the narrow circle of personal thought or a labourer in a thought-factory, but a receiver of knowledge from all the hundred realms of being and free too to choose what it willed in this vast sight-empire and thought empire.[81]

After these three days, Aurobindo returned to Khaserao Jadhav's residence. He noticed that the state of meditation continued effortlessly despite the presence of his friends, that the silence endured in him, that the normal perception of the world had disappeared ... into a strange new condition:

> It threw me suddenly into a condition above and without thought, unstained by any mental or vital

movement; there was no ego, no real world – only when one looked through the immobile senses, something perceived or bore upon its sheer silence a world of empty forms, materialised shadows without true substance. There was no One or many even, only just absolutely That, featureless, relationless, sheer, indescribable, unthinkable, absolute, yet supremely real and solely real. This was no mental realisation nor something glimpsed somewhere above, – no abstraction – it was positive, the only positive reality – although not a spatial physical world, pervading, occupying or rather flooding and drowning this semblance of a physical world, leaving no room or space for any reality but itself, allowing nothing else to seem at all actual, positive or substantial".[82]

Less than five years earlier, on the terrace of a little temple dedicated to Shiva above Srinagar, he had been captured by the vision of a world beyond this world which had transported him into a "strange Unnameable ... An unborn sole Reality world-nude... A Silence that was Being's only word". Then everything had vanished. Now, he experienced permanently that condition of world-abolition. And so he did the only thing he could do: "to accept it as a strong and valid truth of experience, let it have its full play and produce its full experiential consequences until I had sufficient Yogic knowledge to put it in its place".[83] He added: "I cannot say there was anything exhilarating or rapturous in the experience, as it then came to me, but what it brought was an inexpressible Peace, a stupendous silence, an infinity of release and freedom".[84]

Normal reality had been annihilated in what the *Upanishads* call the consciousness of the *silent Brahman*, which Buddhism calls *Nirvana*.

Inspired Political Appeals

Aurobindo had approached Lele to achieve progress in his yogic discipline and liberate his inner energy for the service of his country. Instead, he had come upon the utter unreality of all human activities. When leaving Baroda to address a thousand-strong Nationalist rally in Bombay, he confided to Lele: "How am I going to speak? Not a single thought is coming to me." Lele suggested he present himself by greeting the Divine in the audience with a pranam,* hands joined in a sign of Namaskar, "and the speech will come to you from another source".

Aurobindo heeded the suggestion. He stepped onto the podium and bowed to the audience, clasping his hands. A newspaper title crossed his mind, and a voice – his – started to speak.

His speech kept the audience in suspense for more than an hour. In a clear and concise style, words sprang from his mouth without disturbing the stillness abiding in him. "The whole speech came down from above; not a single thought or expression was mine. It got hold of my organ of speech and expressed itself through it from beginning to end," he would later recall.[85] Exalting courage, disinterestedness, devotion to the Mother, confidence that a Divine Power was at work behind the awakening of national feeling, in an incantatory tone, he had appealed

---
* Movement of inner surrender to the Divine.

to his compatriots to embrace Nationalism as one embraced a religion.

His friends in Maharashtra did not want him to leave. After Bombay, he would proceed to speak at Nasik, Dhulia, Amravati ... nine addresses in the same state of mental inactivity, in the same inspired vein, enthralled the crowds. Words came out slowly, distinctly, without superfluous effect, as he stood motionless, fascinating the audience by the hypnotic charm of his voice. The enthusiasm he generated conveyed volumes about the power of this new art of oratory.

Before leaving Bombay, Lele told Aurobindo: "Surrender yourself to the Divine within and be guided by Him. If you can do that, you needn't do anything else."[86] Aurobindo was grateful to Lele for confirming what would become the rule of his life and the foundation of his Yoga.

All is abolished but the mute Alone.
The mind from thought released, the heart from grief
Grow inexistent now beyond belief;
There is no I, no Nature, known-unknown....[87]

CHAPTER IX

1908

The Bhagavad Gita

Life is not entirely real until it opens into the sense of the infinite.[88]

Silence

A letter from Mrinalini awaited Aurobindo as he arrived in Calcutta. She felt abandoned in Deoghar and expressed her impatience to return to a normal conjugal life. He answered her this sibylline note:

> The state of my mind has at present undergone a change; about that I would not reveal in this letter. Come here, then I will tell you what I have to say. The only thing that can be stated for the moment is that henceforward I am no longer subject to my own will: I must go like a puppet wherever the Divine takes me; I must do like a puppet whatever He makes me do.... You will have to understand that all that I do depends not on my own will but is done according to the command of the Divine. Do not allow anyone to see this

letter for what I have written is extremely secret. I have not spoken about it to anyone but you."[88]

Mrinalini and the faithful Sarojini moved in with him into a new rented house at 23 Scott's Lane. It was spacious enough to accommodate, besides his wife and sister, the indispensable Abinash, who took up his butler-cum-aide-de-camp duties with his customary dedication. Aurobindo returned to his teaching post at the National College, perhaps to earn some money, and resumed his articles for the *Bande Mataram*. He devoted several hours a day to Yoga, receiving occasional visitors, before returning to his silence as soon as they had departed. Abinash watched over the household, managed everyday necessities, and borrowed from the *Bande Mataram* treasurer to supplement the College's meagre pay. Sometimes, he lost his equanimity and affectionately lectured Aurobindo, who met life's every circumstance with the same unfailing serenity, simply smiling at the face of the benign sermonizer.

Aurobindo's writing flowed from complete silence: "it gets itself done without any thought entering my mind or the silence being in the least disturbed or diminished".[89] One day, as one of his colleagues requested the next editorial, Aurobindo, who had not prepared anything, took up a piece paper and began to write. "In this silence that supports the stars,"[90] his words opened up unexpected connections between the convulsions of politics and the hieratic immobility of "That" which abided within him. Fifteen minutes later, he handed over the article. He had not stopped once to think, to cross out words or to revise his page.

Militant Violence

At the end of February, Lele arrived in Calcutta with a disciple. They stayed at Scott's Lane and Abinash recorded in his notebook the effect of this arrival on the meals' frugality. The lunch of rice and lentils was replaced by a boiled potato or a green banana served with a handful of rice. The men observed the day of *puja* by fasting and visiting Ramakrishna's monastery at Belur Math, or they called at the temple of Kalighat to have the *darshan* of the goddess Kali.[91] The household readily complied with this observance of sobriety.

Lele asked Aurobindo if he had followed his recommendations of following the inner voice and meditating twice a day: "When I told him that I had given up meditation – in fact the meditation was going on all the time – he said, 'Ah, the devil has got hold of you.' He did not wait for me to explain anything to him. Since then we began to follow our own ways."[92]

It was Barin who had requested Lele's presence in Calcutta, as he hoped to secure his spiritual guidance for his community at Maniktala Garden.

Owing to the recent government repression, the recruiting at the Garden had made good progress and the dozen or so recruits had become hardened. They were making bombs and Barin plotted to assassinate Governor Fraser, who had replaced Governor Fuller. Because of their clumsiness and failed detonators, however, he and his comrades had to make several attempts before the governor's train finally hit the charge of dynamite destined for him. On 5 December 1907, near Narayangarth in East Bengal, the blast had lifted the locomotive in the air ... without causing the train derailment. Unharmed, the governor had stepped down onto the track to examine the damage and order an investigation.

Shortly before Lele's visit, three group members – Ullaskar Dutt (former student in chemistry and a pyrotechnician), Hemchandra Das (back from Europe with the latest bomb-making technology) and Prafulla – had tested a new explosive mixture with picric acid, which was lighter and more manageable than dynamite. Prafulla was accorded the honour of throwing the test bomb onto a massive rock below the hilltop they had selected. But the mixture, more unstable than expected, exploded in midair, gravely wounding Ullaskar and killing Prafulla on the spot.

It took no time at all for Lele to realise what kind of sports Barin and his friends practiced. He warned them that Yoga and bomb worship were incompatible; that bloodthirsty violence was contradictory to the heart's purification sought by Yoga. However necessary and desirable India's liberation was, it should take place peacefully and without bloodshed.

The young men sneered at him. What! The occupying British would pack their bags of their own accord, without objection and without being impelled to do so – depart India smilingly, as peaceful gentlemen? Who would swallow such a tale? The boys regarded themselves as devotees of the cult of force, worshippers of Kali, the terrible Mother with her garland of human skulls, and not as disciples of the God of love. "You mean they're going to make us dance at the end of a rope?" one of the young men snickered. "It will be much worse than that," replied Lele.[93]

Aurobindo knew what was brewing at the Maniktala Garden. Although Barin often left out the details of his more rugged activities, he made frequent visits to Scott's Lane to keep his brother informed about his plans – and he even stored weapons in the house. Aurobindo tempered the most imprudent initiatives of his younger brother, but he never contradicted his resolve. "It is not wise to check things when they have taken a strong shape, for something good may come out of them,"[94] he would later comment.

Committed body and soul to liberating his country, Aurobindo had confided to Mrinalini: "I know I have the strength to uplift this fallen race; not a physical strength, I am not going to fight with a sword or a gun, but with the power of knowledge.... This is not a new feeling in me, not of recent origin, I was born with it".[95] Against the British occupier, consolidated by two centuries of "enlightened" despotism, he was prepared to condone any means – including force. The sacrifice of his life was a prerequisite he had long accepted, and his brother and the young recruits of the Garden had taken the same oath.

Within the limits of press censorship, he tersely expressed his concept of the political struggle:

> We should be absolutely unsparing in our attack on whatever obstructs the growth of the nation, and never be afraid to call a spade a spade.... Open attack, unsparing criticism, the severest satire, the most wounding irony, are all methods perfectly justifiable

and indispensable in politics. We have strong things to say; let us say them strongly; we have stern things to do; let us do them sternly. But there is always a danger of strength degenerating into violence and sternness into ferocity, and that should be avoided so far as it is humanly possible.[96]

Karmayoga and the War of Kurukshetra

There remained the issue of using violence for a just cause. In his visit to the Garden, Lele had been adamant: spiritual life and war did not mix, even in the case of a war of liberation. He had made it plain that the activities of the young revolutionary recruits were incompatible with the heart's purification sought by Yoga. For him, as for the vast majority of seekers, there was an absolute rule, an impassable gulf between "virtuous" disciples... and the rest.

But was this binary moral principle consonant with the all-governing Spirit of the universe? Aurobindo's thorough investigation into the mysteries of human existence and the ancient wisdoms of his India compelled him to confront himself with this fundamental question – first by recognizing that the world around us does not conform to the spiritual standards of non-violence:

> This world of our battle and labour is a fierce dangerous destructive devouring world in which life exists precariously and the soul and body of man move among enormous perils, a world in which by every step

forward, whether we will it or no, something is crushed and broken, in which every breath of life is a breath too of death.[97]

This realisation was unbearable to the spiritual seeker: "The weakness of the human heart wants only fair and comforting truths or in their absence pleasant fables; it will not have the truth in its entirety because there is much that is not clear and pleasant and comfortable, but hard to understand and harder to bear."[98]

It was Krishna's teaching in the *Bhagavad Gita* which guided Aurobindo in the discovery of "a higher Law by which the soul shall be free from this bondage of works and yet powerful to act and conquer in the vast liberty of its divine being."[99]

In the *Gita*, the symbolic backdrop of this accomplishment was the Kurukshetra Battlefield, during the famous dialogue between Krishna and his friend and disciple, Prince Arjuna. While he was about to engage in a decisive battle for the future of the kingdom, Arjuna's poise was thrown in a turmoil when he realized that he was about to massacre the members of his own clan and family. Overwhelmed by the burden of his conscience, he put his weapons down and turned to Krishna, God incarnate among men, to besiege his help: "Give me a true law, a clear rule of action, a path by which I can again confidently walk."[100]

As time stopped on the battlefield, it is this "true law" that Krishna, verse after verse, taught Arjuna. This was the revelation of Karmayoga, or Yoga of Works. The ultimate exhortation to Arjuna, the crowning of the Yoga, has endured through the ages: *"Abandon all laws of conduct and take refuge in Me alone; I will deliver you from all sin and evil; do not grieve."*[101]

This is the teaching which founded Aurobindo's struggle against the British empire. Instead of withdrawing in Nirvana, of abandoning the phenomenal existence and its conflicts, he found in the Karmayoga of the Gita another way to get involved in the struggle.

Reposing his mind and understanding, heart and will in Him, with self-knowledge, with God-knowledge, with world-knowledge, with a perfect equality, a perfect devotion, an absolute self-giving, he [the disciple] has to do works as an offering to the Master of all self-energisings and all sacrifice.[102]

Like Arjuna, Aurobindo "Abandoned all laws of conduct and took refuge in Me alone", in this inner Divine who whispered of *another* way of feeling, *another* way of acting upon reality. All his activities became subjected to a Will other than his own. In the state of receptive passivity of the Self, he learned to live the divine Omniscience in all circumstances. He spent most of his time initiating himself into this surrender.

Violence and Destruction

How to abandon one's own self in a situation of violence ? Arjuna himself had sunk into utmost despair and perplexity when Krishna directed him to take up the weapons he had abandoned and to resume the fight:

> "I am the eternal Worker within you and I ask of you works. I demand of you not a passive consent to a mechanical movement of Nature from which in your self you are wholly separated, indifferent and aloof, but action complete and divine, done as the willing and understanding instrument of the Divine, done for God in you and others and for the good of the world."[103]

Before Arjuna's incredulous dismay, Krishna then had revealed his terrible face as the universal Destroyer:

> "I am Time who waste and destroy the peoples; lo, I have arisen in my might, I am here to swallow up the nations. Even without thee all they shall not be, the men of war who stand arrayed in the opposing squadrons. Therefore do thou arise and get thee great glory, conquer thy foes and enjoy a great and wealthy empire. For these, they were slain even before and it is I who have slain them; be the occasion only, O Arjuna."[104]

In this final stage of its teaching, the *Gita* is not recommended for everyone. One sees all too well how Krishna's last words might be pressed into serving any sanguinary impulse. This is probably why these passages are generally ignored.

The *Gita* remains a unique teaching in that it dares to view violence and destruction as concomitant with progress and to integrate this difficult truth within the evolutionary march of humanity. Aurobindo's vision ensues:

We have to look courageously in the face of the reality and see that it is God and none else who has made this world in his being AND THAT SO HE HAS MADE IT. We have to see that Nature devouring her children, Time eating up the lives of creatures, Death universal and ineluctable and the violence of the Rudra forces in man and Nature are also the supreme Godhead in one of his cosmic figures. We have to see that God the bountiful and prodigal creator, God the helpful, strong and benignant preserver is also God the devourer and destroyer...

Hence, for Aurobindo, the human fortitude may begin by refusing "to put away the responsibility for all that seems to us evil or terrible on the shoulders of a semi-omnipotent Devil or to put it aside as part of Nature ... or to throw the responsibility on man and his sins, as if he had a preponderant voice in the making of this world or could create anything against the will of God."[105] There remained a sole option: to face God.

It is only when we see with the eye of the complete union and feel this truth in the depths of our being that we can entirely discover behind that mask too the calm and beautiful face of the all-blissful Godhead and in this touch that tests our imperfection the touch of the friend and builder of the spirit in man. The discords of the worlds are God's discords and it is only by accepting and proceeding through them that we can arrive at the greater concords of his supreme harmony, the summits and thrilled vastnesses of his transcendent and his cosmic Ananda [bliss].[106]

Is this law of violence and strife forever part and parcel of our human cycle? A basic constituent of life?

No real peace can be till the heart of man deserves peace; the law of Vishnu cannot prevail till the debt to Rudra [the god of violence] is paid. To turn aside then and preach to a still unevolved mankind the law of love and oneness? Teachers of the law of love and oneness there must be, for by that way must come the ultimate salvation. But not till the Time-Spirit in man is ready, can the inner and ultimate prevail over the outer and immediate reality. Christ and Buddha have come and gone, but it is Rudra who still holds the world in the hollow of his hand.[107]

Fatal Explosion

On 28 April 1908, Aurobindo moved his home to 48 Gray Street. The *Bande Mataram* came out in a new format. As often, its editor pondered the future:

The times are thickening already with the shadow of a great darkness. The destruction of the Congress, begun at Surat, is the prelude for the outburst of the storm that has long been brewing. Great issues were involved in that historic struggle at Surat of which none of the actors were aware…. The fair hopes of an orderly and peaceful evolution of self-government, which the first energies of the new movement had fostered, are gone for ever. Revolution, bare and grim, is preparing her battlefield.... We could have wished it otherwise, but God's will be done.[108]

As if to support this forecast, the new Moderate "Convention" meeting in Allahabad rejected any form of association with the Nationalists. They confirmed the Surat breakup and endorsed the strategy of accommodation with the colonial regime. After a brief debate with his associates, Pherozeshah Mehta had prevailed over "the feeble patriotism and wavering will of the Bengal Moderates".[109]

> The entire Moderate party have agreed to betray the mandate of their country and the future of their people.... No Nationalist henceforth can consent to seek reconciliation with them or clasp the hand that has sold the country for a foreign hire.... It is well. We need waste no further time in seeking a union with the men who before Surat had resolved on a disruption motive by the desire of bureaucratic favour and the fear of bureaucratic displeasure. The day of compromises is past.[110]

At the Maniktala Garden, despite their pyrotechnic failures, Barin and his group continued to hope that their fortune would turn. Since Governor Fraser was now on his guard, a new target had been found in the person of Judge Kingsford. His decision to acquit Aurobindo appeared to be an exception in a magistracy marked by clear-cut support for the government's repression strategy. This judge had sentenced Nationalist journalists to heavy prison terms and ordered the public flogging of a young Bengali man guilty of disrupting his courtroom by shouting "Bande Mataram". To kill him, the pyrotechnicians of the Garden hid a small bomb in a thick legal volume that one of them, disguised as a deliveryman, came to hand over to his servant. The judge, undoubtedly overworked, never had the opportunity to open his "gift". This was fortunate. This time the bomb was well made and the charge of picric acid would have left him no chance.

But for some time now, Barin had been preoccupied with the furtive presences he had spotted around him. Strangers lurked around the Garden and near his brother's house in Calcutta. In fact, the group had been unmasked. Barin and his comrades were unaware that their many attempts against Governor Fraser had allowed the CID to identify them. As early as February 1908, thanks to its spies, the government knew of the Maniktala Garden, Barin was followed everywhere and Aurobindo's house was watched day and night. The chief of police in Calcutta had been ordered not to intervene: the suspects had to be caught red-handed.

Fearing for Judge Kingsford's life, the government had transferred him four hundred miles north of Calcutta and assigned four policemen to guarantee his security. In Muzaffarpur, the judge had resumed his routine at the district court and reorganised his library – still without opening his "gift". Barin decided to take action. At the end of April, he sent two of his men to reconnoitre Muzaffarpur.

On 29 April, armed with a bomb loaded with dynamite, Khudiram Bose and Prafulla Chaki hid outside the clubhouse where Judge Kingsford and his wife had gone for a game of bridge with the wife and daughter of a local barrister. A while earlier, two policemen posted in front of the club had spotted two young Bengalis with suspicious looks, but then they seemed to have vanished into thin air.

When the game of bridge was over and the guests getting ready to leave, each couple called their coach from the porter. Of the two coaches, identical in outer appearance, fate would have it that the vehicle of the two ladies was the first brought to the club entrance. As it pulled out with its passengers and passed the thicket where the two men are hiding, Khudiram ran up and threw his bomb through the open window. It exploded instantly, mortally wounding the two passengers.

In the confusion that ensued, the two assassins fled separately. Khudiram walked all night to the nearest train station. Spotted in the early morning by two gendarmes, he was escorted back to Muzaffarpur, where he confessed to being the bomb thrower. Prafulla was arrested the next day on a train to Calcutta. In the ensuing pursuit, he pulled out a revolver and fired at the policemen, then turned his arm against himself, shooting himself in the head.

Two days later, on 1 May 1908, Aurobindo learnt from a daily newspaper that Police Chief Halliday knew the identity of the perpetrators of the failed assassination attempt against Judge Kingsford. As a precaution, he instructed Barin to remove the weapons from Maniktala Garden and to burn compromising papers. Barin concealed his weapons and explosives with regret, then burned some papers before falling soundly asleep.

PART THREE

Bhakti – Love

Abandoning all laws of conduct seek refuge in Me alone. I will release thee from all sin; do not grieve.

Krishna teaching Arjuna
at the Battle of Kurukshetra

CHAPTER X

1908-1909

Alipore

Prison

On 2 May 1908, before dawn, Aurobindo was jolted from his sleep by the screams of Sarojini rushing into his bedroom. She was pursued by a man with a handgun and the house swarmed with policemen, thirty-five in all, including several British officers. While a very shocked Mrinalini retreated with her sister-in-law, Aurobindo confronted the police officer wielding a search warrant.

As the Gray Street house was searched seven other police squads stormed the homes of Aurobindo's and Barin's relations in Calcutta. Explosives were discovered at friends of Ullaskar's (the group's pyrotechnician) and a manual for bomb-making was found at Hemchandra Das's.

At Maniktala Garden, Barin romantically imagined that he could protect his comrades and his elder brother by claiming to be the sole responsible leader for the group's activities; he guided the police to the cache of arms and explosives. Handcuffed, and with a rope around his waist, Aurobindo was taken to police headquarters, where Abinash and the Bande Mataram staff were already in custody. The police booty secured on this first day was considerable: thirty-three suspects apprehended – thousands of documents plus many weapons and explosives were seized.

Photo of Aurobindo taken in the Alipore prison, 1909

After three days of questioning, Aurobindo understood that the authorities considered him to be the real leader of the group of terrorists. He was transferred to Alipore Jail, the vast, notorious penitentiary south of Calcutta, and kept in solitary confinement pending the hearing of the case. The seriousness of the allegations against him had precluded any possibility of bail.

A fifty-square-foot cell, a metal door with bars overlooking a tiny courtyard encircled by high walls, no window, two coarse blankets, a tin bowl with which to drink, eat, wash, and two baskets coated with bitumen as toilet facilities constituted his new world. His days were now punctuated by morning ablutions in the courtyard, three meals of *lafsi* [rice gruel] and a changing of the guard (to whom he had to answer to confirm that he was still alive).

Aurobindo's inner strength had so far helped him to curb his apprehension of having to face such a situation, but this sudden incarceration affected his spiritual balance: "When I was arrested and hurried to the Lal Bazar Hajat [police station], I was shaken in faith for a while, for I could not look into the heart of His intention. Therefore I faltered for a moment and cried out in my heart to Him, 'What is this that has happened to me? I believed that I had a mission to work for the people of my country and until that work was done, I should have Thy protection. Why then am I here and on such a charge?'"[1]

Yesterday, he had been surrounded by friends, responsible for a newspaper and a political movement – and with meetings and articles to write his days were never long enough. Today, in his small cell, alone, he was experiencing the monotonous, endless hours of solitary confinement:

> In this solitary prison, not having anything else to do, I tried to meditate for a longer period. But for those unaccustomed, it is not easy to control and steady the mind pulled in a thousand directions. Somehow I was

able to concentrate for an hour and a half or two, later the mind rebelled while the body too was fatigued. At first, the mind was full of thoughts of many kinds. Afterwards devoid of human conversation and an insufferable listlessness due to the absence of any subject of thought the mind gradually grew devoid of the capacity to think.[2]

Far from quieting down and lapsing into silence, the mind sank into torpor.

There was a condition when it seemed a thousand indistinct ideas were hovering round the doors of the mind but with gates closed; one or two that were able to get through were frightened by the silence of these mental states and quietly running away. In this uncertain dull state, I suffered intense mental agony…[3]

Time hung heavily. Aurobindo distracted himself by contemplating the tree in his courtyard, gazing at the sky, observing two battalions of warring ants…. He was never afraid of solitude – as long as the solitude was freely consented to – "but here, bound to the wheels of iron law, subservient to the whim of others," he wondered: "Was my mental strength so poor?"[4]

I again sat down to meditate. It was impossible. The intense baffled attempt made the mind only more tired, useless, made it burn and boil.

Despite his acquaintance with the higher planes of poetic intuition, despite the experience of Nirvana which had opened his consciousness to an eternal silence beyond the mind, he found himself overwhelmed, unexpectedly defeated by the most prosaic mental rumination. The power of transcendence of Nirvana could do nothing to alleviate the despotism of this trivially stupid brain activity: the mind was overcome by its own impotence. One day, however, Aurobindo finally managed to seize hold of a thread:

> One afternoon, as I was thinking, streams of thought began to flow endlessly and then suddenly these grew so uncontrolled and incoherent that I could feel that the mind's regulating power was about to cease. Afterwards, when I came back to myself, I could recollect that though the power of mental control had ceased, the intelligence was not self-lost or did not deviate for a moment, but it was as if watching quietly this marvellous phenomenon. But at the time, shaking with the terror of being overcome by insanity, I had not been able to notice that.[5]

This sudden awareness restored the contact with himself by objectifying the irrational phenomenon, by integrating it within his essential self.

> Then I called upon God with eagerness and intensity and prayed to him to prevent my loss of intelligence. That very moment there spread over my being such a gentle and cooling breeze, the heated brain became relaxed, easy and supremely blissful such as in all my life I had never known before. Just as a child sleeps, secure and fearless, on the lap of his mother, so I

remained on the lap of the World-Mother. From that day all my troubles of prison life were over.[6]

Lessons of God

I did not know that God was having a game with me, through which He was giving me a few necessary lessons...[7]

When Aurobindo opened his heart and called for help, the pressure of anarchic thoughts (which the Nirvanic realization had been unable to relieve) was miraculously lifted: a law other than restlessness and disorder had taken over. This was a first "lesson" that the mind was not about to forget. Behind the ordeal he had endured, Aurobindo perceived God's purpose:

> It was to reveal and expose before my mind its own weakness so that I might get rid of it forever. For one who seeks the yogic state, crowd and solitude should mean the same. Indeed, the weakness dropped off within very few days, and now it seems that the mental poise would not be disturbed even by twenty years of solitude.[8]

In his distress Aurobindo had opened himself to a Power that he had not previously suspected: the direct and "personal" intervention of the Divine. The "reversal" he had just experienced within the most obscure and constricted mental consciousness laid the foundation of all the transformations to come.

The other purpose was to give me this lesson that my yoga practices would not be done by my personal effort, but that a spirit of reverence and complete self-surrender were the road to attaining perfection in yoga, and whatever power or realisation the Lord would give out of His benignity, to accept and utilise these should be the only aim of my yogic endeavour.[9]

What he would eventually call "his" Yoga would then become contingent on the surrender of all human deficiencies to the Divine. To abdicate the littleness of the ego and the workings of ordinary nature so that the Divine use them and convert them as He pleased – such was the endeavour Aurobindo would pursue in all fields of existence: mental, vital, corporeal.

This "reversal" would thus become the cardinal event of his future Yoga.

Krishna

Ten days after his incarceration, Aurobindo was allowed to write to his family and to request some personal effects – most importantly, his books, the *Gita* and the *Upanishads*. Then, thanks to a kind doctor's intervention, the prison authorities allowed him two daily walks in the courtyard beyond his door.

Travelling to and fro, I would recite the deeply moving, immortal, powerful mantras of the *Upanishads*, or, watching the movements and activities of the prisoners, I tried to realise the basic truths of the immanent Godhead, God in every form. In the trees, the houses, the walls, in men, animals, birds, metals, the earth, with the help of the mantra: All this is the Brahman, I would try to fix or impose that realisation on all of these. As I went on doing like this, sometimes the prison ceased to appear to be a prison at all. The high wall, those iron bars, the white wall, the green-leaved tree shining in sunlight – it seemed as if these commonplace objects were not unconscious at all, but that they were vibrating with a universal consciousness, they loved me and wished to embrace me, or so I felt. Once in a while, it seemed as if God Himself was standing under the tree, playing upon his Flute of Delight* and, with his sheer charm, drawing my very soul out. The manifestation of these emotions overpowered my whole body and mind, a pure and wide peace reigned everywhere. The hard cover of my life opened up and a spring of love for all creatures gushed from within.[10]

In his minuscule Indian jail cell, Aurobindo was beginning the Yoga of Love or Bhakti Yoga, the third revelation of the *Gita* (after the Yoga of Knowledge and the Yoga of Works):

Afterwards, on many occasions during the period of detention, there arose signs of anxiety, moments of mental unease due to the lack of activity, bodily

---
* Krishna.

trouble or perturbations in the lean periods of yogic life, but that day in a single moment God had given my inner being such a strength that these sorrows as they came and went did not leave any trace or touch on the mind. Relishing strength and delight in the sorrow itself, the mind was able to reject these subjective sufferings.[11]

He summed up his stay at Alipore thus: "I have spoken of a year's imprisonment. It would have been more appropriate to speak of a year's living in a forest, in an ashram, hermitage.... The only result of the wrath of the British Government was that I found God."[12]

It seemed to me that He spoke to me again and said, "The bonds you had not strength to break, I have broken for you, because it is not my will nor was it ever my intention that that should continue. I have another thing for you to do and it is for that I have brought you here, to teach you what you could not learn for yourself and to train you for my work."[13]

The man of flesh and bone could now unlock the natural dynamism of his senses. The Divine was no longer "up above", upon the extreme pinnacle of asceticism and concentration; He was present in everyday life and directed all its activities. The conquest of the Life Divine began.

To raise our whole existence to the Divine Being, to dwell in him, to be at one with him, unify our consciousness with his, to make our fragmentary nature a reflection of his perfect nature, to be inspired in our thought and sense wholly by the divine knowledge, to be moved in will and action utterly and faultlessly by the divine will, to lose desire in his love and delight, is man's perfection.[14]

The Trial

On 18 May 1908, Aurobindo and more than two dozen co-defendants were transferred under escort to the Alipore courthouse. Barely out of the prison compound, the prisoners in the police van began singing, joking and laughing; this joyous mood of the young rebels never abated during the long ordeal of the trial.

As they arrived at the courthouse, the contrast between the rigidity of the guards and mounted police, and the jovial carelessness of the youth walking barefoot, was striking. The reporter of the *Empire* could not hide his surprise: "Not a soul of this gang seems to have the slightest concern!" he exclaimed in his article.

Suspected of "rebellion to overthrow the government" and "armed conspiracy against the King" (the equivalent of high treason), the prisoners were taken to the courthouse every morning and returned to jail every evening after protracted hearings, which often turned into agitated and abusive shouting matches between the judge, prosecutor, attorneys and witnesses.

This preliminary phase of the trial would last five months. It was supervised by Leonard Birley, a young and ambitious magistrate. The Crown was represented by prosecutor Norton, a veteran lawyer from Madras, who was assisted by a group of investigators. In order to establish the charges against each defendant, the proceedings would have to sift through hundreds of testimonies, interview dozens of witnesses, examine and sort through thousands of court exhibits – a labyrinthine ceremonial which prosecutor Norton had devised as an ambush to get his man, namely, Aurobindo.

Before resorting to such a costly process in human and material resources, the authorities had toyed with a simpler alternative for getting rid of Aurobindo: deportation. Andrew Fraser, the governor of Bengal, had long pleaded the case for his banishment to Viceroy Minto: "The man is able, cunning fanatical. He is the leader. He has been in the forefront of all, advising seditious writing and authorising murder. But he has kept himself, like a careful and valued General, out of sight of the 'enemy'. We cannot get evidence against him, such as would secure his conviction in a Court. But we have been fortunate enough to get papers which show his connection with the conspiracy, quite sufficient to convince the reasonable mind and justify deportation. I certainly hope no sentiments will be allowed to prevent this."[15]

But Minto had to take into account the impact that a deportation would have in Britain – the country of the *Habeas Corpus* – especially after the unrest caused by the recent removal of Lajpat Rai, the Punjabi Nationalist leader. So Minto decided to dismiss his subordinate's pleas and to trust his magistrates and his police to unmask Aurobindo.

Aurobindo was silent. His young companions, who for the most part had never seen him before, instinctively showed respect for his quietness. Despite the contrary circumstances, he aspired to deepen his spiritual breakthrough.

The anxiety over the case had vanished from the beginning, now it was a contrary emotion that found room in my mind. God is All-Good, He had brought me into the prison-house for my good, my release and the quashing of charges was certain.[16]

However, he could not completely discard the extraordinary spectacle unfolding before him, at least in the beginning, and it was with an ironical distance that he watched the proceedings: "The nature of the case was a little strange. Magistrate, counsel, witnesses, evidence, exhibits, accused, all appeared a little *outré*. Watching, day after day, the endless stream of witnesses and exhibits, the counsel's [Norton] unvaried dramatic performance, the boyish frivolity and light-heartedness of the youthful magistrate, looking at the amazing spectacle I often thought that instead of sitting in a British court of justice we were inside a stage of some world of fiction."[17]

Norton's endless harangues did not escape his sarcasm: "It was hard to admire his depth of legal acumen – which was as rare as winter in summer. But in the ceaseless flow of words, and through verbal quips, in the strange ability to transmute inconsequential witness into something serious, in the boldness of making groundless statements or statements with little ground, in riding roughshod over witnesses and junior barristers and in the charming ability to turn white into black, to see his incomparable genius in action was but to admire him....

He could create such a wonderful plot by his self-created and abundant suggestion, inference and hypothesis that the great poets and writers of fiction like Shakespeare and Defoe would have to acknowledge defeat before this grand master of the art. It gave me great happiness that Mr. Norton had chosen me as the protagonist of this play."[18]

Aurobindo was no less jocular towards the investigating Judge Birley: "From the start, charmed by Mr. Norton's learning and rhetoric, he had been completely under his spell. He would follow, so humbly, the road pointed out by Norton. Agreeing with his views, he laughed when Norton laughed, grew angry as Norton went angry. Looking at this daft childlike conduct, one sometimes felt tenderly and paternally towards him. Birley was exceedingly childlike. I could never think of him as a magistrate, it seemed as if a school student, suddenly turned teacher, was sitting at the teacher's high desk."[19]

Despite the tumultuous proceedings, Aurobindo tried to keep his focus.

> At first, I tried to continue the inner life while sitting in the courtroom, but the unaccustomed mind would be attracted to every sound and sight, and the attempt would not succeed, in the midst of the noise going on all around. Later the feelings changed and I acquired the power to reject from the mind the immediate sounds and sights, and draw the mind inwards. But this did not take place in the early stages, the true power of concentration had not developed then. For that reason, giving up the futile attempt, I would be content with seeing, now and then, God in all

creatures, for the rest I would observe the words and behaviour of my companions in adversity....[20]

The proceedings would have been utterly boring had they not been vivified by the heckling of the young defendants, their cajoling, their outbursts, their jokes – all of which ultimately pushed the judge to the limit: he threatened to chain them or, even worse, to suppress their meals. The young men then brought books and began reading Bankim Chatterjee's novels, the *Gita*.... The judge then banned the books.

However, it would take more than this to demoralize the young men. Despite the administrative behemoth set in motion to punish them, despite the walls confining them, the chains and the armed guards, they continued to exult in the passion of sacrifice for their country. What will remain for decades in Indian memory is not so much the portentous dramaturgy of the Alipore Bomb Trial as the elastic step and joyful faces of these youths whose innocence carried them beyond the reach of drama and depression.

"Looking at these lads," Aurobindo wrote, "one felt as if the liberal, daring, puissant men of an earlier age with a different training had come back to India. That fearless and innocent look in their eyes, the words breathing power, their carefree delighted laughter, even in the midst of great danger, the undaunted courage, cheerfulness of mind, absence of despair or grief, all this was a symptom not of the inert Indians of those days, but of a new age, a new race and a new activity. If these were murderers, then one must say that the bloody shadow of killing had not fallen across their nature, in which there was nothing at all of cruelty, recklessness or bestiality. Without worrying in the least about the future or the outcome of the trial they passed their days in prison with boyish fun, laughter, games, reading and in discussions. Quite early they had made friends with everyone, with officers, the sentries, convicts, European sergeants, detectives, court officials and without distinguishing between friends and enemies, high and low, had started to tell stories and jokes."[21]

Their joyful vitality ultimately mollified the guards' suspicions. Body searches were skipped; it was almost as guests in a summer camp that the prisoners were returned to their cells every day. The prison visiting room became the scene of amiable encounters with friends and family, who brought fruits and sundry presents, among which were slipped less innocent objects: handguns, for example.

Silence and Yoga

Aurobindo's incarceration became more merciful. The penitentiary authorities showed small acts of kindness toward him. The prison deputy director and the chief medical officer stopped by almost daily "for a little chat". Every other day, the doctor had a milk ration sent from the infirmary to replace the animal mash served as a meal.

This current of sympathy towards a silent detainee demanding neither help nor favour was not due solely to his notoriety, but, as he later explained in a letter to a disciple, to "an instance in which the perception of the

Divine in all, accompanied by an intense experience of universal love or a wide experience of an inner harmony had an extraordinary effect in making all around kind and helpful, even the most coarse and hard and cruel."[22]

Alipore was also an opportunity to feel a common bond with the prison population from the poorest classes, this true India, this Motherland for whom Aurobindo had dedicated his life: "I had felt really happy that no discrimination had been made between the common uneducated masses and myself; moreover, this arrangement added fuel to the flame of my adoration of the Mother. I took it as a marvellous means and favourable condition for learning yoga and rising above conflicts. I was one of the extremists, in whose view democracy and equality between the rich and the poor formed a chief ingredient of Nationalism.... During my stay in the Alipore Jail, I ate, lived, went through the same hardship and enjoyed the same privileges with the other convicts, my fellow nationals, the peasants, iron-monger, potter, the doms and the bagdis, and I could learn that the Lord who dwells in every body, this socialism and unity, this nation-wide brotherhood had put its stamp on my life's dedication."[23]

One of the boys, Naren Goswami, was particularly forward with Aurobindo, always seeking opportunities to speak to him and peppering him with questions. The curiosity of this tall, voluble fellow soon aroused suspicions. His comrades grilled him. Finally he confessed that he had agreed to become a police spy in exchange for his release. However, he swore he had merely intended to deceive the police by providing false information, which would ultimately confuse the prosecution and bankrupt the trial.

It soon transpired that his father, a well-to-do landowner, had also collaborated with the police to help in the release of his son. The main issue now was whether or not Goswami would corroborate Norton's thesis about Aurobindo's explicit role as the head of the conspiracy.

In mid-June, hearings were suspended while the prisoners were transferred to a large common cell. All were ecstatic at being reunited, singing and laughing long into the night. Aurobindo isolated himself as best he could.

Goswami foolishly boasted that he was the one behind the transfer. At first, the others refused to talk to him, then they feigned co-operation by disclosing fanciful names of members of the conspiracy. Goswami hastened to pass on these names to the police, who then launched a wild goose chase for these would-be new conspirators.

Aurobindo remained silent. Withdrawn in a corner of the vast hall, he tried to preserve his spiritual poise, lest the company of others would affect the inner state of detachment and peace he had attained.

I did not understand that for the fullness of my spiritual experience it was necessary to evoke opposite emotions, hence the Inner Guide suddenly deprived me of my dear solitude, flung me into the stream of violent outward activity.[24]

In the daytime, he worked on his Bengali, instructed his companions on the fundamental concepts of British justice, coached them to reflect on morality and immorality in politics, on anarchism and imperialism.... Sometimes, he even enjoyed impersonating prosecutor

Norton while Ullaskar (the pyrotechnician) imitated Judge Birley.

Outside of these lively exchanges, he remained in concentrated silence, the very intensity of which imposed a distance and a respect, while the striking fixity of his black eyes seemed to contemplate a far-off world.

With wind and the weather beating round me
  Up to the hill and the moorland I go.
Who will come with me? Who will climb with me?
  Wade through the brook and tramp through the snow?

Not in the petty circle of cities
  Cramped by your doors and your walls I dwell;
Over me God is blue in the welkin,
  Against me the wind and the storm rebel.

I sport with solitude here in my regions,
  Of misadventure have made me a friend.
Who would live largely? Who would live freely?...[25]

"When he smiles," one of the young men commented, "there is no muscle contraction like with us; the smile is in the eyes." They also notice his black shiny hair, as if lustred in oil, while theirs dried up in the parched air of the prison. One of them gathered his courage: "Do the guards give you oil in secret?" Aurobindo smiled: "The practice of Yoga has caused some bodily changes. My hair uses the fat directly from my body."

After his morning ablutions, Aurobindo maintained a headstand [*Salamba Sirsasana*] for several hours. One day, while in this posture, the Governor of Bengal made an unannounced visit. Receiving no reaction to his presence, he watched awhile and finally, after half an hour, left the room without uttering a word.

Sometimes, it seemed to the boys that Aurobindo's body was an independent, detachable object, while he himself was "elsewhere." They remembered the particular occasion when, in an act of provocation, a huge Scottish Highlander had grabbed Aurobindo, thrown him across his shoulders and twirled him about with affected hilarity. Aurobindo had remained inert, without a trace of emotion or irritation – as if he were not the twirling body. The giant then had quickly ceased his provocation, resting him on the ground without a word.

Another day, one of the boys became emboldened to ask, "What do you get by the practice of Yoga?" Aurobindo put an affectionate hand on the young man's shoulder: "I got what I was looking for."[26]

Executions

The court hearings resumed after a one week suspension. Norton promptly announced that Naren Goswami had agreed to become a prosecution witness in exchange for his pardon. His deposition would last until the first week of July. He narrated at length his enlistment in the secret society in 1906, his meeting with its leaders, Aurobindo and Jatin Banerjee,* and the revolutionary activities in which he had taken part. He pointed to Aurobindo in the courtroom. He further disclosed the

---

* Whom Aurobindo had sent to Calcutta when he was laying the foundations of the revolutionary uprising in Bengal.

names of other unsuspected members of the conspiracy, who were immediately apprehended for a further trial session.

As a man of action, Barin refused to accept that his destiny be determined by a police informer. Escape seemed to be the best answer to Goswami's betrayal. Some guns had been secured during the prison visits, and Barin had devised a plan of escape, even contemplating taking to the hills to raise an army to continue the fight. His enthusiasm had already converted some of his comrades to his program, but before implementing it, he had to inform his brother. Aurobindo listened quietly but replied that, for his part, he intended to face the judgement.

On 13 August, the defendants were called one by one to the bar to make a personal statement. Aurobindo abstained from any declaration. Most detainees did the same. The next day, following customary procedure, two defence lawyers requested to cross-examine Naren Goswami, Norton's star witness. Pressed by the government to complete his hearings, which had already dragged on too long, the judge rejected their request. On 15 August, the lawyers tried again. Again, Birley refused to grant their request.

On this particular 15 August, Aurobindo celebrated his thirty-sixth birthday. All the inmates wore broad smiles on their faces. To the correspondent of the *Empire*, who did not conceal his astonishment at the defendants' joyous mood, one of them pointed to Aurobindo, whose face, "hitherto grave and prepossessed, had been metamorphosed into one of sprightliness and sunniness."[27] To the intrigued reporter, Aurobindo explained that since 1906, his birthday had always coincided with striking phases of India's march to Independence: from the inauguration of the National College to the trial of the *Bande Mataram*, and today, thanks to these ongoing legal proceedings, the development and propagation of a revolutionary movement*. "You can add to those coincidences the fact that I shall very probably be coming back from the Andamans** on my birthday next year," he concluded with a facetious smile.

Finally, on 19 August thirty-one defendants were formally charged with "acts of war against the King". On the basis of Goswami's testimony, Aurobindo was suspected of being one of the instigators of the conspiracy. This made him liable to lifetime deportation.

Pending the actual trial, the defendants were to be held in detention until the second batch of suspects, arrested on the basis of Goswami's denunciations, passed through Birley's court. All were returned to their cells, except for Goswami, who was transferred to the European Quarter to shelter him from possible reprisals.

Unbeknownst to Aurobindo, the most determined of his companions had devised a plan to eliminate Goswami, who was rumoured to be preparing a new denunciation of Nationalist sympathizers. They believed it had become vital to silence him. Satyen Bose, one of Aurobindo's relatives known for his experience with guns, would attract the traitor by offering to turn himself into

---

* It is also on 15 August (1947) that India regain her freedom from the British.
** One of the British penitentiaries located in the Andaman Islands in the Indian Ocean.

a prosecution witness. On the morning of 31 August, Goswami agreed to leave the protection of the European Quarter to go to the prison hospital, where Satyen Bose, flanked by Kanailal Dutt, awaited him. The two prisoners were armed with revolvers. After a scuffle and a wild chase on the prison grounds, Goswami was shot and killed.

Outside their cells, the inmates heard the gun shots. When the siren blared, they could not contain their joy. Aurobindo remained impassive and silent.

Pandemonium erupted at Alipore. Following a meticulous body search, all the prisoners were transferred to individual cells with nothing but the clothes on their backs. A squad of armed Highlanders was requisitioned to stand guard day and night with shoot-on-sight orders. Visits and articles from outside were prohibited, as were books and personal exchanges among prisoners.

Satyen Bose and Kanailal Dutt were deferred to a special Court of Justice. Before the judge, Kanailal, who had fired the deadly shot, acknowledged his role, invoking Goswami's betrayal to justify the execution. He was sentenced to hang and did not appeal the verdict. Satyen, initially exonerated by a mixed jury, was also sentenced to the gallows after the public prosecutor obtained the review of his trial before a higher court.

In October, Kanailal's execution aroused immense emotion in Bengal. Even the *Times* of London reported the slow procession of his remains through the streets of Calcutta, strewn with rice and coins. To prevent the risk of a popular uprising, Satyen Bose's remains were discreetly incinerated in the prison compound and his ashes scattered in secrecy.

One of the youngest members of Barin's group, Nolini Kanta Gupta (who would later become one of Aurobindo's closest disciples and the secretary of his Ashram), did later acknowledge that Kanailal and Satyen had shot Goswami to save Aurobindo.

Spiritual Explorations

Aurobindo was undoubtedly the only prisoner in Alipore not to deplore the new drastic regime imposed after Goswami's assassination. A new period of solitude began.

What happened to me during that period I am not impelled to say, but only this that day after day, He showed me His wonders.[28]

He would not say more about his growing intimacy with Krishna. Many years later, however, he was content to illustrate his discoveries of so-called miraculous powers with a few examples:

I had a questioning mind: "Are such siddhis as utthapana [levitation] possible?" I then suddenly found myself raised up in such a way that I could not have done it myself with muscular exertion. Only one part of the body was slightly in contact with the ground and the rest was raised up against the wall. I could not have held my body like that normally even if I had wanted to.[29]

Called *utthapana*, these powers of levitation, cultivated by the fakirs of legends, aim at circumventing the influence of physical forces such as gravity. For example, Aurobindo practised keeping his arms in the air without muscular contraction. He succeeded so well that he fell asleep in this position – until he was suddenly awakened by the screams of the guard who thought him dead. Although he had no intention of becoming a fakir, he was determined to investigate the body's unusual abilities. He experimented with the power of *anima* [lightness], which awakens the body's internal dynamism and liberates it from inertia; for example, eliminating tiredness as one eliminates an importunate thought. He practised sleeping one day out of three, then decided to fast for ten days, "to see what happens".

A sudden flash of intuition opened his eyes to pictorial art:

> Suddenly one day in the Alipore jail while meditating I saw some pictures on the walls of the cell and lo and behold! the artistic eye in me opened and I knew all about painting except of course the more material side of the technique.[30]

One day, the experiment involved the bites of red ants. Why should the body feel these bites as painful? He tried to reverse the current of pain and verified that "pain and pleasure are a convention of our senses":

> At first we can gain [release from pain] in two ways by suffering. One is, we learn to bear it; and the other we find something in us which does not suffer. When we

have got the separation we can learn the way to transform it into Ananda [bliss].[31]

Within the fifty square feet of his cell Aurobindo not only broadened his mental horizon beyond Cartesian logic. From unfathomable abysses to vertiginous heights, he probed invisible worlds; without losing his critical sense he beheld visions:

> There are many kinds of visions. Some visions are only images, some are forms taken by our vital desires, or they are images of mental thoughts. Often they are our own creations; they do not correspond to any Truth. True visions are very rare and they can't be completely understood unless one had the right discernment and great purity in the being.[32]

Perhaps the most fruitful and important experience of this period was his encounter with Vivekananda's spirit. For two whole weeks, the great Vedantist (who had died six years earlier) manifested himself to him in his meditation, imparting an intimate knowledge of previously unsuspected higher planes of consciousness he would call the "Supermind":

> It was the spirit of Vivekananda who first gave me a clue in the direction of the Supermind. This clue led me to see how the Truth-Consciousness works in everything. He didn't say "Supermind". "Supermind" is my own word. He just said to me, "This is this, this is that and so on.... He visited me for fifteen days in Alipore Jail and, until I could grasp the whole thing, he

went on teaching me and impressed upon my mind the working of the higher consciousness – the Truth-Consciousness in general – which leads towards the Supermind.[33]

The Judgement

On 19 October 1908, reporters jostled each other at the doors of the Alipore courthouse. Armed Highlanders cordoned off the van from which the defendants were extracted one by one before being shoved into the courtroom. The conspirators of Maniktala Garden were about to stand trial.

Aurobindo had not left his cell for six weeks. Rumours about him had abounded. The endless hours of meditation, the lack of sleep, the insufficient nourishment and the strange postures of his body had caused his codefendants to feel anxious. Although pale and thin, Aurobindo climbed down from the van and took a few steps outside. His dhoti clasped around the waist in the manner of a common man, a shawl thrown lightly over his shoulder, his face wore the look of an untroubled child.

As the packed courtroom audience rose to greet the presiding judge, Aurobindo immediately recognized him. Charles Porten Beachcroft, who had been appointed to rule on the fate of the group of revolutionaries, had been a fellow student in the Indian Civil Service. They had often met, especially in Greek classes, where Beachcroft had come in second behind Aurobindo, and during Bengali tests where Beachcroft had got the higher marks.

They had then lost sight of each other, the judge climbing the ranks of the magistracy, while Aurobindo had become the main figure of Nationalist opposition in Bengal.

All the same, this new phase of the trial was nothing more than a tedious repetition of the previous exercise with Judge Birley. The same witnesses repeated the same statements, the same fifteen hundred documents and the same pieces of evidence were again examined under a microscope. This time, however, Norton was hampered by the lawyers who cut short his most fantastic flights of imagination and compelled him to minimum legal constraints.

No fewer than fifteen lawyers represented the defendants. They were paid from the defence fund set up to cover Aurobindo's legal expenses. His Uncle, Krishna Kumar, had launched a national fund-raising campaign through his newspaper, the *Sanjivani*. The appeal, written and signed by Sarojini, was then relayed by other newspapers, which ended up collecting several thousand rupees from Indian and foreign donors. The government was put on alert and searched of the *Sanjivani's* premises for the list of contributors. But the expectation of a miraculous catch fell flat when the police realised that the kitty was made up of modest donations from thousands of anonymous Bengalis.

Shared among thirty-five defendants, the defence fund was still not large enough to pay for the services of the legal ace who had agreed to represent Aurobindo. This man soon declined his assistance because of the insufficient funds. A shattered Krishna Kumar then resolved to appeal to Chittaranjan Das, a less experienced lawyer and supporter of the Nationalist party, who agreed to take on the case. The trial, which would last another six months, now began in earnest.

The crime of "conspiracy and acts of war against the King" carried the death penalty. All the defendants pleaded "not guilty". Norton found no difficulty in connecting the Garden's youth to acts of violence, but the task of implicating Aurobindo was far more challenging. Norton was unrelenting. The trial turned into a one-man witch hunt.

The prosecution possessed only two scribbled notes of Barin's which were presumed to associate Aurobindo with the violent activities of the group. One of the two notes used the word "sweets" as a plausible code reference to bombs. The other "written proof", exhumed by overzealous policemen, were brushed aside by Charles Porten Beachcroft, a man who knew his job and prided himself on a keen sense of British justice. In this spirit, he ruled that Birley had acted improperly in refusing the cross-examination of the prosecution witness, Goswami. He declared Goswami's testimony inadmissible.

But Norton did not admit defeat easily. He dragged the proceedings on until the following March. Brandishing documents and court exhibits, recalling every witness who had already testified, he obstinately tried to convince Beachcroft of Aurobindo's responsibility.

Aurobindo had to refute Norton's arguments one after the other. He had welcomed with relief the arrival of his friend Chittaranjan Das in the defence team and slipped notes and instructions to him on the best way to respond to the prosecutor. But suddenly, an inner voice ordered him to rely exclusively on his lawyer: "This is the man who will save you from the snares put around your feet. Put aside those papers. It is not you who will instruct him. I will instruct him."[34]

From then on, Aurobindo cut himself off from the surrounding circumstances of his trial:

> I looked and it was not the Magistrate whom I saw, it was Krishna, it was Krishna who was sitting there on the bench. I looked at the Prosecuting Counsel and it was not the Counsel for the prosecution that I saw; it was Sri Krishna who sat there, it was my Lover and Friend who sat there and smiled. "Now do you fear?" He said, "I am in all men and I overrule their actions and their words.... I am guiding, therefore fear not. Turn to your own work for which I have brought you to jail and when you come out, remember never to fear, never to hesitate. Remember that it is I who am doing this, neither you nor any other."[35]

The High Court of History

An ominous rumble of anger and discontent stirred through Bengal. The Alipore Trial and harshness of government repression had unleashed a cycle of mounting violence in the people. Governor Fraser escaped an umpteenth attempt against his person; the policeman who had arrested Prafulla Chaki after the failed attack on Judge Kingsford was shot dead in Calcutta; a police spy involved in another case was found decapitated. Presuming to defeat the rising popular outrage, the government of Bengal resorted to deportation: nine Nationalist leaders, including Aurobindo's uncle, his friend Subodh Mallik and several other collaborators of the *Bande Mataram* were deported without trial. The Secretary of the Interior later admitted: "We would have deported him too [Aurobindo] if he had not already been in prison."[36]

The prisoners' treatment became more severe. They were now chained to each other in the courtroom and locked in a kind of wire-mesh cage. The British press was moved by these measures. The Secretary of the Interior justified them by the climate of tension spreading through the country which demanded extra precautions against terrorists. Undaunted, Norton pursued his mission, a loaded pistol close at hand on his table. When, in February, a gunman entered the courthouse and killed the prosecutor of an adjacent trial, a shaken Beachcroft adjourned the session for the day.

In March, after examination of all the court exhibits, Norton finally presented his concluding arguments. This lasted for yet another two weeks. Then it was the turn of the defence lawyers to deliver their conclusions. They denied implicitly the existence of any organized "conspiracy" against the Crown, arguing that Aurobindo's articles were uniquely freedom calls for his country and for his people. Chittaranjan Das read a statement by Aurobindo:

> If it is suggested that I preached the ideal of freedom to my country, which is against the law, I plead guilty to the charge. If that is the law here, I admit having done it and I request you to condemn me. It is for that that I have given up all the prospects of my life. It is for that that I came to Calcutta to live for it and to labour for it. It has been the one thought of my waking hours, the

dream of my sleep. If that is my charge you can chain me, imprison me, but you will never get out of me a denial of that charge.

Chittaranjan Das then proceeded to demonstrate that most of the documents presented by the prosecutor were forged and that the testimonies of the police informers were lies. He concluded his pleading with these words:

> My appeal to you, therefore, is that a man like this who is being charged with the offences imputed to him stands not only before the bar in this Court but stands before the bar of the High Court of History and my appeal to you is this: That long after this controversy is hushed in silence, long after this turmoil, this agitation ceases, long after he is dead and gone, he will be looked upon as the poet of patriotism, as the prophet of Nationalism and the lover of humanity. Long after he is dead and gone his words will be echoed and re-echoed not only in India but across distant seas and lands.[37]

Finally, on 5 May 1909, the very day Aurobindo entered prison one year ago, Beachcroft read out his judgement. Police reinforcements were mobilized to cordon off the neighbourhood and guard the roads. Aurobindo was completing one year of incarceration.

The judgement upheld the ruling of a conspiracy against the British Crown and inflicted upon each defendant a punishment commensurate with the degree of his involvement. Fifty of its three hundred pages were devoted to Aurobindo alone, "whom more than any other the prosecution are anxious to have convicted and but for his presence in the dock there is no doubt that the case would have been finished long ago." After an in-depth analysis of Aurobindo's public and private writings, Beachcroft concluded that the evidence "falls short of such proof as would justify me in finding him guilty of so serious a charge as a member of the conspiracy." The judge did not perceive in his writings any incitement to violence, only the promotion of ideas of freedom and a regeneration of his country. The handwritten note of the "candies" (the sole contentious point) was not held against Aurobindo. Indeed, would Barin have used the words "My dear brother" to write to Aurobindo when all Bengali men address their elder brothers as "Sejda"? Furthermore, written in Surat when the two brothers were attending the Congress session, the letter would have had to follow Aurobindo throughout all his moves and travels, finally to be found by the police five months later in a house on Gray Street into which he had just moved. Beachcroft refused to buy Norton's fabrication.

Barin and Ullaskar Dutt were condemned to the gallows. Ten men directly involved in acts of violence were sentenced to life deportation in the Andaman Islands. Eight men were condemned to lesser terms of imprisonment. All the others, including Aurobindo, were acquitted and released straight away.

His liberation was as if the material validation of Krishna's teaching: *"Abandon all laws of conduct and take refuge in Me alone; I will deliver you from all sin and evil"*.

.

CHAPTER XI

1909-1910

The Karmayogin

Slackening of the Nationalist Movement

Depending on their leanings, political observers were either aggrieved or elated, but all were astounded by Aurobindo's acquittal.

If the revolt against the British government could be called a conspiracy, then Aurobindo was not only one of its main figures but also a leading driving force. Without him, Barin would not have been able to organize his forces. It was Aurobindo's passion which had inspired the young revolutionaries; it was his rousing and vibrant *Bande Mataram* chronicles which had sustained the Nationalist fervour. The British officials who had pleaded for his deportation had understood this, and were furious that he had slipped through the net.

Upon his release Aurobindo received a standing ovation from the Calcutta lawyers gathered to celebrate his acquittal. His discharge emphasized his position as a major opponent to the colonial regime, and the latter's determination to bring him down. Since Beachcroft's judgement was legally unassailable, the government would have to find another way of undermining his influence. The British archives testify to the flurry of growing concern aroused in the ministries by the man whom the Governor of Bengal now called "the most dangerous man with whom we had to deal."[38] Communications between Ministers and Secretaries of State reflected their alarm. Despite the trial fiasco, this man had to be stopped at all costs. But how? Deportation was now their preferred choice. He just needed to be watched until a favourable pretext to catch him arose – for example, while he delivered a subversive speech.

Spies were assigned to follow his every movement. His travels outside Calcutta were monitored; his public appearances were preceded by instructions to the local authorities to break up audiences wanting to hear him. The post office near his home was infiltrated by a team of CID agents charged with opening and copying every letter he sent or received.

Mrinalini could not be subjected to the tensions of this besieged life; her nerves would not have withstood another police raid. Although she had found solace and protection with her family during Aurobindo's imprisonment, these times of crisis were a nightmare for her. An old friend of her father's in Calcutta offered her accommodation, while Aurobindo moved to his uncle's house, where his Aunt Lilavati, very distressed by her husband's incarceration, gratefully accepted the reassuring simplicity of his presence.

There, at 6 College Square, in an upstairs room converted into an office, he spent his first month of freedom receiving strings of visitors eager to see and touch the man who had escaped the gallows. All were stunned by the smile in his eyes. Sometimes, as if by contagion, their eyes lit up with a similar light of clairvoyance. Rabindranath Tagore himself was mesmerised by this man over whom life's dramas seem to have no hold – who had returned from prison looking younger than when he went in.

For the anonymous contributors to his defence fund Aurobindo published a message of gratitude: "... If it is the love of my country which led me into danger, it is also the love of my countrymen which has brought me safe through it."[39]

This month of rest confirmed what he had felt in prison: the slackening of the Nationalist movement. The government's repressive apparatus had been enhanced with new legislations which empowered a single magistrate to outlaw a newspaper. As a consequence, both *Yugantar* and *Bande Mataram* had been forced to close down and many *Samitis* had been driven underground.

The movement had also lost most of its leaders – above all, Tilak. After the attempt on Justice Kingsford's life, Tilak had been charged and prosecuted for an article rejecting the responsibility for terrorism on "the exasperation produced by the autocratic exercise of power by the unrestrained and powerful white official class."[40] He was sentenced to six years of banishment to Burma for sedition. A letter by Secretary Morley to Viceroy Minto shed light on the sham of his trial: "It is certain that they will obtain his [Tilak's] condemnation for the jury has obviously been made to measure; it is certainly not the Goddess of Chance who produced this astonishing result of seven Europeans, two Parsees, and no Hindu."[41]

Nine other Nationalist leaders (including Aurobindo's uncle and his friend Subodh Mallik) were in jail. Lastly, his two close companions in arms, Bepin Chandra and Lajpat Rai, had voluntarily exiled themselves to England and America – most probably to escape Tilak's fate.

Repression had rarefied the crowds and cooled the early enthusiasm of the Swadeshi boycott. Discouragement and apathy had returned. To further their advantage Secretary Morley and Viceroy Minto concocted a new set of "popular" reforms, the goal of which was to scatter a few crumbs of advisory power to the same, unchanging Indian notables.

What remained of the Congress after the Surat explosion was merely a rubberstamp assembly for English policy, tightly controlled by the Bombay Mehta-Gokhale clique. At its December 1908 Madras session, its president had declared: "When in the fullness of time the people have outgrown the present system of administration," they might hope for "the extension to India of the colonial form of self-government, though this ideal can only be realised in the distant future."[42] Emboldened by the Nationalist collapse, Gokhale had added: "Only madmen outside an insane asylum could hold the idea of India's independence as an ultimate goal. It is an insane idea, a criminal idea."[43] *Pax Britannica* savoured its triumph.

Uttarpara Speech

Since coming out of jail, most people Aurobindo had encountered seemed lost and bewildered. "When I went to jail, he said, the whole country was alive with the cry of Bande Mataram, alive with the hope of a nation, the hope of millions of men who had newly risen out of degradation."[44]

Everything had now changed. A hush had fallen on the country. "What shall we do next? What is there that we can do?" people asked.

Like a Gilgamesh bringing the knowledge of Immortality from his journey to the Kingdom of the Dead, Aurobindo was to attempt to revive his countrymen's spirit and convey his faith in a higher destiny than that of eternal submission. On 30 May 1909, he agreed to deliver a public speech at the cultural association of Uttarpara, north of Calcutta.

He spoke about himself as he had never done before. He confessed to his initial distress in prison, his questions, the oppression of solitude, the assault of anarchic thoughts flooding his brain. He then disclosed his prayer and the response that ensued – his liberation – Krishna's presence in his heart; doubts and uncertainties swept aside, the "proof" of the divine reality behind human disguises.

Six hundred people held their breath.

He finally put forward that the experience in his solitary cell was analogous to the ordeal sustained by the country. As he had to endure the barrenness of silence in prison, "so it was the same power which had sent down that silence... so that the nation might draw back for a moment and look into itself and know His will."[45] For him as for the evolution of the country, it was vital to link spiritual reality with daily material life, what he called "the two ends of existence" – Spirit and Matter – so they harmonise within the same order of existence. Then India could rise again and regain her freedom for the service of the world.

The next day, his entire speech was reproduced in the Calcutta press.

If his audience had been able to open themselves to the truths he articulated, the collective determination of the country would undoubtedly have been strengthened. In the absence of which, Aurobindo continued alone to steer the course between "the two ends of existence".

The Karmayogin

He returned to work.

Taking advantage of his notoriety, he combined the dynamism of public meetings with that of his pen, travelling from towns to villages to address appreciative audiences. The *Bande Mataram* having foundered in the morass of the recent press laws he launched two new weekly newspapers under his sole editorship: *The Karmayogin* (in English) and the *Dharma* (in Bengali).

The *Karmayogin* cover displayed an engraving of Krishna driving Arjuna's war chariot at the battle of Kurukshetra. Although dedicated to spirituality, literature, science and philosophy, the *Karmayogin* did not refrain from "noticing current events only as they evidenced, helped, affected or assisted the growth of national life and the development of the soul of the nation."[46] With the *Karmayogin*, Aurobindo extended the theme of his Uttarpara speech:

> We aim not at the alteration of a form of government but at the building up of a nation. Of that task, politics is a part, but only a part.... We believe that it is to make the yoga the ideal of human life that India rises today. It is a spiritual revolution we foresee and the material is only its shadow and reflex.[47]

The "spiritual revolution" he envisioned had nothing to do with temples or the fragrance of incense – it would first and foremost shake the mirages of the materialistic dogma. He called out to the young:

> We say to the individual and especially to the young who are now arising to do India's work, the world's work, God's work, "You cannot cherish these ideals, still less can you fulfil them if you subject your minds to European ideas or look at life from the material standpoint. Materially you are nothing, spiritually you are everything.... First therefore become Indians. Recover the patrimony of your forefathers. Recover the Aryan thought, the Aryan discipline, the Aryan character, the Aryan life. Recover the Vedanta, the *Gita*, the Yoga. Recover them not only in intellect or sentiment but in your lives.... You must win back the kingdom of yourselves, the inner *Swaraj*, before you can win back your outer empire.[48]

He thought of humanity, particularly of Western materialism and the predicament which all modern European societies faced: the unbridled race towards a "progress", which could never capture the meaning to life.

We say to humanity, "The time has come when you must take the great step and rise out of a material existence into the higher, deeper and wider life towards which humanity moves. The problems which have troubled mankind can only be solved by conquering the kingdom within, not by harnessing the forces of Nature to the service of comfort and luxury, but by mastering the forces of the intellect and the spirit."[49]

The Two Ends of Existence

With the first issue of the *Karmayogin* barely in print Aurobindo left Calcutta for a new tour in East Bengal. In the train to Khulna, he immersed himself in the inner world. The next day, in the steamer taking him to Barisal, he practised ocular concentration on the solar disk [*trataka*], which stimulated the subtle senses. Lights and images with shimmering colours flashed before his closed eyes, an unknown voice was heard, a current of well-being bordering upon ecstasy ran through his body. The presence of Krishna permeated the atmosphere, while a blue-black bust of Kali, topped by a sun, loomed.

He flowed with the experience. Sometimes, for a few minutes, he entered a state of wakeful trance [*Samadhi*], then the mind resumed its normal activities. Some time before reaching Barisal, he distinctly heard Krishna's voice within his heart: "I come to slay [the ego]."[50]

He noted everything. Although he never put up any resistance to the experience, he managed not to lose himself in it. He methodically recorded the detail of each perception or sensation: its intensity and stability, its impact on material life and extension to other ranges of consciousness.

> I think I can say that I have been testing day and night for years upon years more scrupulously than any scientist his theory or his method on the physical plane.[51]

When landing on the mainland at Barisal, he was taken to the temple of Kali where he immediately felt the Presence in the image of the divinity. During nearly a week of encounters, speeches and meetings with town audiences and political activists, he continued to record the movements of his inner life. He now seemed capable of going effortlessly from the inner focus to the outer.

> If one attains to a condition in which one can do these things only with the surface of the consciousness, keeping inside and observing what is done on the surface, but not forgetting oneself in it, then the poise is not lost. But it is a little difficult to get at this duplication of oneself – one comes to it however in time especially if the inner peace and calm become very intense and durable.[52]

In his first speech at Jhalakati, evoking the drama of a young local man who had been deported for his political opinions, Aurobindo confronted head on an atmosphere of profound discouragement in the audience. He exhorted his compatriots to remember *who* they were, to reconnect with the ancestral source of their strength:

> We are a people ancient as our hills and rivers and we have behind us a history of manifold greatness, not surpassed by any other race.... We are a people to whom suffering is welcome and who have a spiritual strength within them, greater than any physical force. We are a people in whom God has chosen to manifest Himself more than any other at many great moments of our history. It is because God has chosen to manifest Himself and has entered into the hearts of His people that we are rising again as a nation...

As he did at Uttarpara, instead of dwelling on the wickedness of the colonial regime, he urged the audience to dwell on the spiritual dimension of the ordeals India was being put through:

> I saw the striding of the storm-blast and the rush of the rain and as I saw it an idea came to me. What is this storm that is so mighty and sweeps with such fury upon us? And I said in my heart, "It is God who rides abroad on the wings of the hurricane, – it is the might and force of the Lord that manifested itself and His almighty hands that seized and shook the roof so violently over our heads today...." Repression is nothing but the hammer of God that is beating us into shape so that we may be moulded into a mighty nation and an instrument for His work in the world. We are iron

upon His anvil and the blows are showering upon us not to destroy but to re-create.[53]

After this speech, he noted in his journal: "All relics of fear, disgust, dislike, hesitation rapidly disappearing. Doubt checked, suspension of judgement."[54]

In a single month, he delivered six speeches in the same vein before returning to Calcutta for a final address at College Square. His smiling ease, the mix of casual humour and flame in his unrehearsed words subjugated the crowds. He alone could evoke India's destiny with this simplicity and credibility while dispelling fears and summoning the energy of the future. Everywhere he inspired the crowds. They felt he lived his words.

Police spies continued to follow him everywhere; his every word was noted down, then studied under a magnifying glass. The organizers of the meetings where he was to appear were often threatened with reprisals. All branches of government, from Viceroy Minto on down, were determined to silence him. The Secretary of State wrote to his colleague of the Interior: "I would not hesitate to deport Aurobindo if he cannot be silenced in any other way. If he is allowed to go on, he will very soon have the country in a blaze again. We should certainly have deported him last December."[55]

Minto was inclined to prosecute him: "Aurobindo is again on the warpath. I only hope he will commit himself sufficiently for us to be able to prosecute."[56] A speech delivered in Calcutta, in which Aurobindo had stated that "being imprisoned for a just cause was not intolerable," was scrutinised by government lawyers. They concluded that the phrase smacked of sedition, but then it had to be printed to be challenged in court. Unfortunately for them, the statement was not published in the *Karmayogin*, so the legal sleuths had to try something else. While intimidation and repression had worked against the leaders of the Nationalist movement – all of whom had more or less backed down or else been removed from the political stage – Aurobindo did not bend. On the contrary, he seemed to derive energy from the force used against him. Worse, the arrows of his wit ridiculed the authorities and filled the *Karmayogin* readers with glee:

> Since the initiation of the Swadeshi movement, the army of spies and informers have grown as plentiful as insects round a bright light....The office of the *Dharma* has recently been favoured with the loitering of watchers who spend their days gazing lovingly at the building and making affectionate and importunate enquiries as to the movements and habits of the editor. This open lovemaking strikes us as a little indecent; it would be better done behind a veil. And what do the authorities hope to gain by these unique researches? Do they hope to see either bombs or packets of sedition being carried into the building?... Even a bureaucracy ought to credit its political opponents with some little common sense.[57]

Menace to Freedom

As he repeatedly stated, Aurobindo favoured the full political integration of Muslims into the Indian nation for which he prayed:

> We do not shun, we desire the awakening of Islam in India even if its first crude efforts are misdirected against ourselves.... Of one thing we may be certain, that Hindu-Mahomedan unity cannot be effected by political adjustments or Congress flatteries. It must be sought deeper down, in the heart and the mind, for where the causes of disunion are, there the remedies must be sought.[58]

However, it was the role and future of India in the world that gave rise to his most impassioned articles. He sketched a scenario in which India would ultimately stand as a last resort against the cataclysm precipitated by the collective egoism:

> Either India is rising again to fulfil the function for which her past national life and development seem to have prepared her, a leader of thought and faith, a defender of spiritual truth and experience destined to correct the conclusions of materialistic Science by the higher Science of which she has the secret and in that power to influence the world's civilisation, or she is rising as a faithful pupil of Europe, a follower of methods and ideas borrowed from the West....[59]

At the end of July 1909, Sister Nivedita, who had kept some contact in the British administration, warned him that his deportation had been decided upon. She advised him to leave the country immediately and take refuge abroad. Instead, he chose to face up to the threat with his only weapon: his writing. On the 31st of July, he signed a long article in the *Karmayogin* entitled "An Open Letter to My Compatriots."[60] Conceived as a political testament, this essay once again hammered away at the articles of faith of the Nationalist agenda, laying the foundations for an autonomous administration which would take into account the political situation of the country.

> Our ideal of Swaraj involves no hatred of any other nation nor of the administration which is now established by law in this country.... They lie who say that this aspiration necessitates hatred and violence. Our ideal of patriotism proceeds on the basis of love and brotherhood and it looks beyond the unity of the nation and envisages the ultimate unity of mankind. But it is a unity of brothers, equals and freemen that we seek, not the unity of master and serf, of devourer and devoured....

How to build a national identity without calling into question the legality of the British administration? It was necessary, he wrote,

> ...to unite and organise ourselves in order to show our efficiency by the way in which we can develop our industries, settle our individual disputes, keep order and peace on public occasions, attend to questions of

sanitation, help the sick and suffering, relieve the famine-stricken, work out our intellectual, technical and physical education, evolve a Government of our own for our own internal affairs so far as that could be done without disobeying the law or questioning the legal authority of the bureaucratic administration, this was the policy publicly and frankly adopted by the Nationalist party.

In this programmatic text, Aurobindo outlined the approach that would challenge the British administration in the march of India towards its independence the next forty years. How much time would have been saved, what suffering and blood spared if some bold or enlightened minds among British leaders had paid attention and grasped his words? After his departure from the political stage, it would fall to Gandhi and his followers to apply the precepts that he summarized here. Unfortunately, Gandhi's doctrinal rigidity and the inconsistency of some of his political initiatives (his incomprehensible surrender to Muslim demands) would blur the directness of the ideas developed by Aurobindo; his "program" would become bogged down by the conceit and fanaticism of non-violence.

He prefaced his essay with this statement: "Rumour is strong that a case for my deportation has been submitted to the Government by the Calcutta Police and neither the tranquillity of the country nor the scrupulous legality of our procedure is a guarantee against the contingency of the all-powerful fiat of the Government watchdogs silencing scruples on the part of those who advise at Simla [the Viceroy's summer residence]."

He speculated that the government would not risk inflaming British opinion by resorting to extra-legal practices but would choose caution and wait for a more favourable opportunity to eliminate him. Reckoning that his new notoriety as a well-known opponent complicated the task of the authorities, Aurobindo played on his status as "public enemy number one".* This *Karmayogin* article removed, at least for now, the threat of deportation.

Rise of Terrorism

Bengal was about to celebrate the fourth anniversary of the boycott of 1905, and the "Open Letter to My Compatriots" was at the centre of all political conversations in Calcutta. On 7 August, in Greer Park, Bhupendranath Bose, a Moderate leader, occupied the platform before a sparse audience. As *The Times* correspondent noted, "A public speaker in England would regard such a gathering as almost an insult. The remarkable fact was, however, that dampened as the crowd was, it burst into loud cheering when Mr. Aurobindo Ghose was seen standing nearby. He was unquestionably the hero of the meeting."[61] As Aurobindo proceeded to the podium, Bhupendranath,

---

* To illustrate the difference that reputation could confer on a litigant in the colonial system, we cite the case of this obscure publisher of a Madras newspaper, A.B. Kolhatkar, who had the unfortunate idea of publishing certain articles of the *Bande Mataram, after the Beachcroft Court had examined them and found them non-seditious*. Accused of disseminating "seditious" material, this man was sentenced to 15 months in prison, including five in solitary confinement with chains. Even the demands of explanations by members of Parliament in London would not elucidate the arbitrariness of his punishment.

who had promised the authorities not to let him speak, abruptly declared the meeting over.

The collaborationist strategy of the Moderate party was moribund. Still, a few local leaders, such as Surendranath Banerjee, escaped being entirely discredited by playing both sides of the fence. But other loyalists did not take such precautions. In a speech in Poona, Gokhale condemned all who called British hegemony into question. He seethed against Nationalists ("madmen worthy of the insane asylum"), against the idea of independence ("a criminal ideal that can only lead to more repression and violence"), against the strategy of passive resistance ("a cover used by men to save their skin"). He did not mention Aurobindo by name, but it was clear he had him in mind. Gokhale concluded his broadside by charging Nationalism with the acts of terrorism that had plagued society for months. A sensational political assassination gave new ammunition to his argument.

Less than a month ago, a twenty-six-year-old Indian, Madanlal Dhingra, had shot and killed William Curzon Wyllie, aide-de-camp to Secretary of State Morley. This assassination had been all the more shocking because it was perpetrated in broad daylight in London, where the Dhingra was studying engineering. He justified his action by the desire to offer himself as a "sacrificial martyr" to avenge his country. He was condemned to death and hanged on 17 August.

In India, the Anglo-Indian press exploded with hysterical imprecations against the Nationalists. Yet the Nationalist precept of sacrifice had nothing to do with killing Englishmen at home as an expiatory tribute! In the *Karmayogin*, Aurobindo squarely placed the assassination committed by Dhingra in the category of irrational acts: "No man but he can say what were the real motives for his deed.... Minds imbued with these ideas [of martyrdom] are the despair of the statesman and the political thinker. They follow their bent with a remorseless firmness which defies alike the arrows of the reasoner and the terrors of a violent death.... Here his country remains behind to bear the consequences of his [Dhingra] act."[62]

Copycat acts of terrorist violence broke out in the country. This imitative spell of Barin's methods sparked yet more government repression, thus reducing further the space for Nationalist opposition. In the *Karmayogin*, Aurobindo again expressed his disapproval of acts of anarchic and disorderly violence claiming to restore the country's freedom: "The outbreak of Terrorism compels us to restrict our circle of passive resistance lest even by the most peaceful rejection of unjust laws we should seem to be encouraging lawlessness and disorder."[63]

On 15 August 1909, he celebrated his thirty-seventh birthday. A large group of friends and admirers came to congratulate him; as the crowd quickly became too large for his uncle's small house, they gathered in the street beneath his balcony to express their affection, offering fruits and sweets while singing "Bande Mataram". He thanked them with these words, recorded by a police spy, who described him as visibly touched: "Always be patient. Never give up hope. Instability, impatience are the great problems of our nation. When you have a great purpose before you and a firm resolution in you, no difficulty, no matter how great, can divert you."[64]

Last Involvements

Co-opted members of the institution the British and their loyalist allies continued to call the "Indian National Congress" prided themselves on having no Nationalists in their ranks. The political coterie that epitomized them, led by the old Mehta-Gokhale pair, headed toward its fated demise. By contrast, in Bengal, the confrontation still went on to determine which side, Moderate or Nationalist, would embody the future political orientation of the province. In the beginning of September, the Hooghly Conference was the backdrop for a new altercation between the two camps. Aurobindo, head of the Nationalists, faced the old Moderate champion, Surendranath Banerjee.

As usual, the Moderates had selected the venue of the conference, Hooghly, where they controlled the Hosting Committee. As usual, too, they had covertly rewritten the resolutions voted on at previous conferences in order to mitigate their impact. But this time they no longer held a majority. Yet Aurobindo was determined to avoid an irrevocable split. He and his friends submitted resolutions rejecting the superficial political reforms planned by the government, but they were met with a stubborn refusal to extend the boycott as a measure of economic salvation. Tumult rose up in the assembly. Aware of their new strength, the Nationalist delegates appealed to the spirit of Surat. Surendranath, the conference president, shrugged his shoulders in mute despair....

As the assembly visibly drifted towards chaos Aurobindo stood and raised a hand to demand silence. Since the Moderates refused to comply with the boycott, he recommended the path of conciliation – but... "at the same time we want it to be clearly understood that in taking this course we are not for a moment receding from the policy and line we have taken up."[65] He asked the Nationalist delegates to abstain from voting against the Moderate resolution and to leave the hall in silence in protest. Astounded Moderate delegates watched the orderly withdrawal of those impetuous youths led by a man hardly older than themselves.

In his conference report published a few days later, Aurobindo explained: "The Nationalist party is in practical possession of the heart and mind of Bengal. It is strongly supported in other parts of India and controls Maharashtra. It is growing in strength, energy and wisdom. It surely inherits the future. Under such circumstances, it can afford to wait."[66] An overt break had been avoided, leaving the future open.

Aurobindo then journeyed to Silhet, on the River Surma, for a tour to the far-flung Eastern districts of Bengal, where he could measure the radical transformation which had occurred. Everywhere, he and his friends were welcomed with open arms. All shared the same aspiration for freedom and independence and, in a single voice, the conference on the Surma voted resolutions far more progressive than the Hooghly conference. Everyone now also acknowledged Aurobindo as a Yogi whose charisma stemmed from the light radiating from his being. After his closing speech on self-help and passive resistance, which he delivered in an English which few could comprehend, the audience left the communal hall with smiles on their faces, gratified by the sight of the peace emanating from the speaker.

Returning to Calcutta in mid-September, Aurobindo received a correspondent of *India*, the Nationalist weekly from South India. As he saw the discreet figure waiting for him in the small room, the reporter paused in the doorway: "Is this the Yogi destined to liberate us by a radical transformation, to show a new way for India?" But then his eyes met Aurobindo's: "Oh, what knowing in these eyes! What grace in them! What peace! The whole room exuded peace." He asked Aurobindo to speak of his vision in prison of Krishna, for "the *Darshan* of the Supreme is a rarity in this age." When Aurobindo responded, the combination of humility, solemnity, innocence and the light on his face dissipated the journalist's last doubts: "Yes, I saw Krishna. I had all my visions in a waking state: they were not dreams." Asked about the Yoga he had practised during his imprisonment, Aurobindo replied: "It was Bhakti Yoga. Leave all responsibility to the Divine. Try to realize that whatever you think, speak, or do is not yours, and that it is the Divine who thinks, speaks and acts through you. Crush your ego; be without the 'I'"[67]

The 16th of October, the anniversary of the 1905 Bengal Partition, was drawing near and Aurobindo was eager to celebrate it not as a day of partition, but as a day of unity. In the three speeches he delivered on this occasion, he emphasised this unity, "only dimly symbolised in the ceremony of the *Rakhi*,* a unity which cannot come into

---

* Multicoloured thread bracelets which Indians tied to each other's wrists regardless of the class or community to which they belonged.

being until a perfect comradeship in aspiration, in struggle, in suffering shall have been created throughout the length and breadth of the land: Indian fraternity based on Indian liberty and Indian equality."[68]

The British, however, had not given up undermining relations between Muslims and Hindus. One of the schemes of the new reform plan was to separate Muslim electoral representation from the rest of the population. The partition of Bengal had aimed at diluting Hindu influence by redrawing the map of the province. The goal was now, through an electoral process presented as a democratic advance affirming the rights of a minority against the overwhelming Hindu majority, to generalize the polarization to the entire country. Aurobindo retorted that the plan ought to have also considered the other minorities: the Parsees, Sikhs and Christians, for example. "Under modern conditions, India can only exist as a whole,"[69] he repeated emphatically:

> We will not for a moment accept separate electorates or separate representation, not because we are opposed to a large Mahomedan influence in popular assemblies when they come, but because we will be no party to a distinction which recognises Hindu and Mahomedan as permanently separate political units and thus precludes the growth of a single and indivisible Indian nation.[70]

It followed that Nationalism had to be above denominational choices, that the Indian nation had to be founded on a basis of secularism. He strongly repudiated the notion of Hindu Nationalism and called instead for a

Hinduism refreshed at the source of the Vedanta, aware of its spiritual power, conscious of mankind's essential oneness, but declining to found its existence on a supremacy or a rivalry with other denominations, including Islam. It would be in failing to adhere to this golden rule of separation between civil and religious identities – especially under Gandhi's leadership – that India would suffer its greatest tragedies in the decades to come.

The country, the *Swadesh*, which must be the base and fundament of our nationality, is India, a country where Mahomedan and Hindu live intermingled and side by side.... Our ideal therefore is an Indian Nationalism, largely Hindu in its spirit and traditions, because the Hindu made the land and the people and persists, by the greatness of his past, his civilisation and his culture and his invincible virility, in holding it, but wide enough also to include the Moslem and his culture and traditions and absorb them into itself.[71]

He tirelessly reaffirmed that faith and courage would conquer all difficulties – "faith that looks beyond all momentary obstacles and reverses and sees the goal that God has set before us, and the courage that never flinches for a moment but moves forward calmly, wisely, but strongly and irresistibly to that goal."[72]

Aurobindo spent most of his days working in the *Karmayogin's* office, never losing sight of his inner research.

As for concentration and perfection of the being and the finding of the inner self, I did as much of it walking in the streets of Calcutta to my work or in dealing with men during my work as alone and in solitude.[73]

At his uncle's, he received a visit from Ramsay MacDonald, the leader of the British Labour Party and future British Prime Minister, who noted in his journal: "I called on one whose name is on every lip as a wild extremist who toys with bombs and across whose path the shadow of the hangman falls. He sat under a printed text: 'I will go on in the strength of the Lord God'; he talked of the things which trouble the soul of man.... He was far more of a mystic than a politician. He saw India seated on a temple throne. But how it was to arise, what the next step was to be, what the morrow of independence was to bring – to these he had given little thought. They were not the nature of his genius."[74]

As a consequence of his meeting with Aurobindo, Ramsay MacDonald was one of the very few British politicians to voice his sense of the perverted waste in human resources stemming from Westminster's unbridled policies. As his intervention in Parliament on 28 April 1910 made clear, "I feel perfectly certain that unless the India Office will insist upon its officials administering India with some generosity, some catholicity of sentiment and some serious attempt to associate with themselves men like Mr. Aurobindo Ghose, the future is going to be very much darker than it is at present."[75]

Political Swamp

Aurobindo was now alone in maintaining the course of Nationalist fervour in the treacherous waters of the regime's repressive policies. He drew his strength and insights from the innermost depths of his heart, which he felt as the source and prospect of all the world's movements, including his own. The thunder rambling around him, the threats to his freedom and security, the growing burden of responsibility, all became reconciled and resolved within this sacred shrine. He could return there again and again – restore his peace, find his bearings, and quench his thirst. *That* held the key to the future. It was the source from which he poured his vision of a liberated future into a tormented reality. He aspired to replace the fixation on servitude in the hearts of his compatriots with a different prospect: India recovering her strength and her true spiritual nature, the fulfilment of a divine intention.

Meanwhile, his notoriety became increasingly intolerable to the authorities. "I attribute the spread of seditious doctrines to him personally in a greater degree than to any other single individual in Bengal, or possibly in India,"[76] the new Governor Baker wrote in private correspondence to the Viceroy.

That his political opponents spared no effort to muzzle him was, after all, fair game. But a stealthier antagonism raised its head: the jealousies of the political swamp. Those who had turned their devotion to India into a profession of faith, and sometimes into a gainful profession, took umbrage at his notoriety. Without loosing his sense of humour, Aurobindo responded to the "reproaches" of

Surendranath, the old Moderate leader, who now called him "an impatient idealist":

> The reproach of idealism has always been brought against those who work with their eye on the future by the politicians wise in their own estimation who look only to the present.... The advice to wait is valueless unless we know what it is that we have to wait for and why it is compulsory on us to put off the effort which might be made at the present. If we can progress quickly there must be adequate reasons given us for preferring to progress slowly or to stand still. We have not yet heard those adequate reasons.[77]

The cause of the gulf between Aurobindo and a certain Bengali intellectual elite was that he had left behind the intellectual perception of the world. "He thinks himself divinely guided," wrote a caustic Nivedita, "but religious experience and strategy have nothing in common and should not be mixed."[78] Even his silence was assailed as it seemed to confirm this "otherness". He maintained that he was not turning his back on reality – as evidenced by his daily involvement in the public struggle – yet he was secretly reproached for being "above" things. His lack of personal ambition was suspect.

He did not dwell upon or respond to these criticisms. Twenty-five years later, he would mention them only laconically: "I have been so blackened by human judgements that I do not wish to be guided by them in judging others."[79]

The Noose Tightens

When the appointments to the new Councils introduced by the recent Morley-Minto reforms were made public, the worst fears were confirmed. The confessional affiliation sought by the administration had largely benefited Muslims to the detriment of Hindus. Far from easing tensions this amplified community discord which would culminate in 1947 with the creation of the separate country of Pakistan. The Moderates had supported the reforms and profited from the largesse of the regime.

Even in Bengal, Aurobindo must recognise that the Moderates would never accept Nationalists among them. His own conciliation efforts ran counter to Surendranath's demand (prompted by the Mehta-Gokhale script) for a "creed" of good conduct prior to any Nationalist participation. This "creed", which Aurobindo equated to a yoke, was unacceptable. He finally resolved: "We regret to announce to the country that there is not the least possibility of having a united Congress."[80]

> The period of waiting is over. We have two things made clear to us, first, that the future of the nation is in our hands, and, secondly, that from the Moderate party we can expect no cordial co-operation in building it. Whatever we do, we must do ourselves, in our own strength and courage.[81]

While all reasonable options seemed to vanish one after another, he took a final stock of the country's political situation, reiterating his faith in a harmonious evolution of society:

The perfect self-fulfilment of India and the independence which is the condition of self-fulfilment are our ultimate goal. In the meanwhile such imperfect self-development and such incomplete self-government as are possible in less favourable circumstances, must be attained as a preliminary to the more distant realisation. What we seek is to evolve self-government either through our own institutions or through those provided for us by the law of the land.[82]...

Published in the *Karmayogin* on 25 December 1909, this article, "To My Countrymen," which he made into a second open letter to his compatriots, marked a final appeal to reason to all Indian political classes. Like the preceding articles, however, it fell on deaf ears. The government lawyers seized upon it to flesh out new arguments in order to prosecute Aurobindo. And inevitably he was charged – for the third time.

The beginning of 1910 brought no respite to the Nationalists. Even the project of national education did not escape the downturn. The National Council of Education, of which Aurobindo had been a founding member in 1906, brazenly betrayed the ideals upon which it had been founded. Using the pretext of declining popular support during the boycott celebrations in Calcutta, the Council leaders forbade students to attend.

Aurobindo gave vent to his indignation: "It is only the crowning act of a policy by which they are betraying the trust reposed in them by the nation, contradicting the very object of the institution and utterly ruining a great and salutary movement."[83]

The only good piece of news came from the Alipore Court of Appeals: two judges commuted the death sentences of Barin and Ullaskar to deportation for life. A third detainee was acquitted and released while eight others had their prison sentences reduced. In congratulating the judges for their patience during the hearings and the fairness of their arbitration, Aurobindo commented that "death sentences for political crimes only provide martyrs to a revolutionary cause, nerve the violent to fresh acts of vengeance and terrorism, and create through the liberation of the spirits of the dead men a psychical force making for further unrest and those passions of political revolt and fierceness to which they were attached in life."[84]

Since Alipore, although he was enduringly popular with the young, Aurobindo had kept his distance from violent revolution. His visibility as the head of the Nationalist party made his involvement impossible, but above all, the time of the *Yugantar* and terrorism was over. He felt that "so long as young men are attached to these methods of violence, the efforts of a more orderly though not less strenuous Nationalism to organise and spread itself must be seriously hampered."[85]

Yet blind terrorism did not abate in the least. In November, Viceroy Minto narrowly escaped a bomb thrown by a stranger in Ahmedabad. A month later, members of a Maharashtra group fired at a magistrate in Nasik and killed him. At the end of January, inside the Alipore courthouse, a young Bengali shot Detective Shamsul Alam, whom Aurobindo had encountered during his arrest. From London, Paris, Berlin and New York, new revolutionary propaganda spread into the Indian emigrant community. Based in Geneva, a newspaper called "Bande Mataram" campaigned to criticize the editorial line of the late original *Bande Mataram* as well as its editor.

The government turned its wrath against the Nationalist party, blaming it for its moral responsibility in fostering acts of terror. Once again, Aurobindo's voice rose to denounce the executive short-sightedness: "The disease is one that can only be dealt with by removing its roots, not by denouncing its symptoms. The Anglo-Indian papers find the root in our criticism of Government action and policy and suggest the silencing of the Press as the best means of removing the root.... Our idea is that it will only drive the roots deeper: to silence Nationalism means to help Terrorism."[86]

In February, yet again, the government toughened the press laws. Publishers had now to deposit a bond before writing the first line – a surety which would be sequestered, along with the newspaper, at the slightest editorial misconduct. Aurobindo took note of the new regulations, which targeted above all the publications with the most modest means: one step closer toward total censorship. Rumours of a new deportation project circulated within the police departments. This time it would involve removing twenty-four political opponents, including Aurobindo. In fact, the highest authorities of the Government of India had agreed upon a list of fifty-two names in addition to his own: almost all of the declared opponents of Bengal, with the exception of the most inoffensive members of the Moderate party.

Standing aside

It became impossible to express a contrary opinion. The Anglo-Indian press, a long-time ally of the British, did not hold back its scathing attacks against the Nationalist party. This Aurobindo denounced:

> If the *Englishman* is tired of assassinations, we also are tired of the thankless and apparently unsuccessful task of regulating popular discontent and pointing out legitimate paths to national aspiration on the one hand and attempting to save the officials from themselves on the other. We have only persevered in it from a strong sense of our duty to the country. But we are beginning to feel that Fate is more powerful than the strongest human effort. We feel the menace in the air from above and below and foresee the clash of iron and inexorable forces in whose collision all hope of a peaceful Nationalism will disappear, if not for ever, yet for a long, a disastrously long season.[89]

In February 1910, terrorist violence further intensified, and repression fell indiscriminately upon the Nationalists. Aurobindo warned the government:

> A very serious crisis has been induced in Indian politics by the revival of Terrorist outrages and the increasing evidences of the existence of an armed and militant revolutionary party determined to fight force by force. The effect on the Government seems to have been of a character very little complimentary to British statesmanship. Faced by this menace to peace and security

the only device they can think of is to make peaceful agitation impossible.... If free speech, if free writing, if free association is made impossible under the law, it is tantamount to declaring a peaceful Nationalism illegal and criminal.[90]

Taking into account the consequences of this further disintegration and since British leaders refused to seize upon the peaceful opportunity of a genuine national regeneration, he decided to withdraw from political action. Before doing so, he addressed the government one last time:

> The one, the only remedy for the difficulties which beset them [the government] in India, is to cease from shutting their eyes on unpleasant facts, to recognise the depth, force and extent of the movement in India, the radical change that has come over the thoughts and hearts of the people and the impossibility of digging out that which wells up from the depths by the spades of repression. They are face to face with aspirations and agitations which are not only Indian but Asiatic, not only Asiatic but worldwide.

Finally, he addressed his compatriots to explain his intention to leave politics:

> Revolution paralyses our efforts to deal peacefully but effectively with Repression; Repression refuses to allow us to cut the ground from under the feet of Revolution. Both demand a clear field for their conflict. Let us therefore stand aside, sure that Time will work

for us in the future as it has done in the past, and that, if we bear faithfully the burden of the ideal God has laid upon us, our hour may be delayed, but not denied to us for ever.[92]

Taking Stock

Aurobindo's appeals to resolve the contradictions of colonial hegemony by relying on a reasoned Nationalism were not heard.

A few years later, other Indian leaders would take up the torch pursuing the strategies he had formulated in the *Bande Mataram* and *Karmayogin*, but his voice and inspiring vision would be sorely missing.

Not until 1947, after her direct involvement in two world wars and the massacres unleashed by the creation of Pakistan, would India finally recover her independence and freedom to manage her own affairs. But the country would be forced into dismemberment presented as a propitiatory offering to Muslim territorial ambitions by a British leadership only too glad to extricate itself from the quagmire which it had played such a major role in creating. In the euphoria prevailing amidst the Allied victory over the Axis powers, the Indian tragedy went largely unnoticed – all the more so since the bloodbaths at the Indo-Pakistan border were overshadowed by the seductive diversion offered by Gandhi's pacifism and non-violence.

Nevertheless, the colonial disengagement of England was hailed as a model of "moderation" and "humanity". A few erudite scholars at a later date had the audacity to credit the former colonial power with the seventy years of "peace and democracy" that India has known since her independence.

Although the notorious vices of colonialism are now buried in the mists of time, we must return for a moment to the blindness of British policymakers in India. Incapable of perceiving the elements of greatness or nobility in a civilization other than their own, the British abandoned themselves to the illusion of their racial supremacy. In their hands, even the proverbial English "liberalism" bore the marks of an additional Machiavellianism to achieve their self-serving ends.

Viceroy Minto was a perfect example of the men who had ruled over India for three centuries. In the speech he made in January 1910, to install the famous Council that was to grant consultative powers to a select few Indians, he declared: "We have distinctly maintained that representative Government in its Western sense is totally inapplicable to the Indian Empire and would be uncongenial to the traditions of Eastern populations – that Indian conditions do not admit of popular representation – that the safety and welfare of the country must depend on the supremacy of British administration – and that that supremacy can, in no circumstances, be delegated to any kind of representative assembly."[93]

Such was the mindset of the governing elite of a country that would be dubbed, after its independence in 1947 and until recently, "the world's greatest democracy".

That none of these men – with the notable exceptions of Judge Beachcroft and the future British Prime Minister MacDonald – ever paid the least attention to the voice of Aurobindo, who strove ceaselessly to put forward so many practical solutions for an organized and peaceful transition towards a free and integral India, speaks volumes about their arrogant blindness.

Aurobindo was not alone in embodying his country's popular aspirations – India was far from lacking in remarkable and courageous men – but his voice was unique in its inspiration and lucidity, in its faith and the dynamism of its vision and ideals. In spite of Aurobindo's four years of uninterrupted presence on the political stage, in spite of his hundreds of articles and dozens of highly inspired speeches received by passionate audiences, the only relationship that British officials ever had with him was that of game hunters pursuing their prey: his words were searched for forensic evidence to incarcerate him, never to understand him.

Chandernagore

At the beginning of February 1910, the *Karmayogin* refrained from any further political commentary. Its columns were now filled with articles on literature (a translation from the original Bengali of *Anandamath*, Bankim Chandra's banished novel), on art (*The National Value of Art*) or on Yoga (*Yoga and Human Evolution*). Aurobindo sometimes added his own poetry and his translations of the *Upanishads*. He still spent his days working in the newspaper's office and in the evenings, a few Alipore veterans, as had been their custom while in prison, joined him to chat or to improvise lectures on history or literature.

On the 11th of February, Aurobindo went to Howrah Railways Station to greet his uncle. To a rousing ovation, Krishna Kumar Mitra returned to Calcutta after fourteen months at Agra Prison. A few days later, Aurobindo would again be present at the harbour to welcome a former *Bande Mataram* colleague, Shyamsundar Chakraverty, returning from deportation in Burma.

That evening, the usual congenial circle at the *Karmayogin* was interrupted by the agitated arrival of a young man, Ramchandra Majumdar, who warned of Aurobindo's imminent arrest. He had just learned from a police officer, a member of his family, that an arrest warrant had been issued and that the police were about to swoop down on the *Karmayogin* premises. While everyone began commenting animatedly upon this alarming news and debating what to do – some even proposing physically confronting the police – Aurobindo himself remained silent, motionless. Then suddenly, he stood up and declared that he was leaving immediately. Later, he explained that he had heard an inner voice which he knew very well, pronounce the following three words: "Go to Chandernagore".*

The small group left the *Karmayogin* office and hastened through the maze of narrow alleyways leading to the pier at the Hooghly River. They soon reached their destination, descended the steps leading to the river and hailed a small boat with two rowers. Two young men, Biren and Moni, boarded the craft with Aurobindo.

---

* About twenty miles north of Calcutta, on the Hooghly River, the small French colony of Chandernagore [15 sq. miles] was enclosed within British India.

Published through an intermediary, Aurobindo's last words in the *Karmayogin* evoked yet again the conditions of his country, emphasising what was still needed to carve out a path to freedom:

> In all the events of the last year and a half [since his release from Alipore] the voice of the divine Teacher can be heard crying to us, "Abandon that you may possess; do my will and know yourselves, purify yourselves, cease to follow your fancies." He that has ears, let him hear. Knowledge will not come without self-communion, without light from within, not even the knowledge of the practical steps that can lead to success. Every step that is taken in the light of a lower wisdom will fail until the truth is driven home.

He concluded this last article by invoking the memory of the glorious departed souls from the previous century and their contribution to India's awakening and ultimate liberation:

> The work that was begun at Dakshineshwar [by Ramakrishna] is far from finished, it is not even understood. That which Vivekananda received and strove to develop, has not yet materialised.

Then, lifting the veil upon a future that had yet to utter its last word:

> A less discreet revelation prepares, a more concrete force manifests, but where it comes, when it comes, none knoweth.[95]

Perhaps the words of the historian R.C. Majumdar best encapsulated Aurobindo's fleeting journey through Indian politics: "His emergence in Indian politics was as sudden as it was unexpected; of him, it may be truly said that he came, he saw, and he conquered. He rose like a meteor and vanished like it from the political atmosphere. But unlike the meteor, the dazzling light he shed on Indian politics did not vanish with him. The torch which he lighted continued to illuminate Indian political firmament."[94]

CHAPTER XII

1910
Departure

The Vedic Rishis

The night was spent rowing up the river in silence. The small boat glided through the darkness with the rhythmic sweep of the oars. This departure from Calcutta was no accident. The menace of an arrest had been in the air ever since he came out of prison. Given the prevailing atmosphere, it had become futile to continue mediating between two kinds of deafness: the intransigence of the British regime and the fanaticism of terrorism. The sky paled with the first hint of dawn as the little craft approached its destination. The only person Aurobindo knew in Chandernagore was a former Alipore inmate, a respectable man whose misfortune had been to be included in one of Naren Goswami's lists. Charuchandra Roy was a sincere believer in the liberation of India, but did not have the mettle to fight. Hauled before the Alipore Court, he had not fared well in prison. After his release, gained through a guarantee from the French authorities in Chandernagore, he had gone back to his life as a high school teacher, pledging never again to meddle in "politics". Biren's sudden, unexpected knock on his door thus filled him with terror. He declined to receive Aurobindo, suggesting that he take refuge in France....

Perhaps to make up for his defection, Charuchandra communicated the news of Aurobindo's arrival to another member of the group of Nationalist sympathizers. Biren, who kept watch on deck, soon spotted an individual timidly approaching the boat. Sensing that he was observed, the man drew closer. When Biren informed him that the boat came from Calcutta, he asked: "Would Mr. Aurobindo be on board?" This unknown individual was called Motilal Roy and, having heard of Aurobindo's presence, had rushed to offer his services.

"How can you help me? Would it be possible for you to put me up?" asked Aurobindo straightaway. Motilal replied that he would give his life if necessary! "I came to receive you... I will personally take care of everything." Aurobindo scrutinized his face, smiled, then asked: "How far do you live?" Motilal directed the boatman to a *ghat* a few cables' length upstream. Before following his new host Aurobindo asked Biren and Moni to return to Calcutta to inform Sister Nivedita about the unexpected turn of events and to ask her to take charge of the *Karmayogin* publication.

This new departure, less outwardly dramatic than that of Alipore, would lead to an infinitely more radical change in Aurobindo's life.

The room that Motilal had put at his disposal was rudimentary. Aurobindo sat silently on the floor and withdrew within himself. When Motilal returned several hours later, he found him still sitting in the same position, staring upwards. "He has utterly resigned himself to God," thought the young man. Motilal had never before met anyone like Aurobindo: "When he talks, words come out of his mouth as if by someone else made him speak. If his hand moved, it is controlled, as it were, by a third agency."[96]

Aurobindo's stay in Chandernagore lasted for a month and a half. To insure his security, a few of Motilal's friends took turns hiding him. But even in a simple thatched hut, where he was given only dried fruit, he maintained his concentration.

After arriving in Chandernagore Aurobindo noticed that his visions had become more frequent. Legible characters and alphabets now formed before his eyes, as if superimposed in the air. This phenomenon [*akasha lipi*] was repeated every day – finally revealing that these cryptograms were a transcription of past, present or even future events. The "memory" in the invisible world did not seem to distinguish between the tenses: the future may easily coexist with the past or the present. Aurobindo, who sensed a rare receptivity in Motilal, confided to him: "The gods of the invisible world become visible. They are as significant as the alphabet, and want to communicate something which I endeavour to discover."[97]

Another realm of investigation now aroused Aurobindo's interest. His daily concentration often led him to a peculiar inner zone of complete opacity. What power greater than the searching mind could penetrate this darkness? For days on end, he continued to run into an impassable threshold. Then, finally, he received a response in the guise of three divine figures from the ancient Indian tradition. Well-known to Yogis, Ila, Saraswati and Sarama personify three levels of the powers of intuition: revelation, inspiration and intuition itself. Aurobindo realised that these faculties of clairvoyance would help him to plumb the depths and mysteries of the subconscious.

The three goddesses whose light illuminates the cave of the "Powers of Darkness" are figures from India's Vedic heritage: they date back to an age prior to the *Upanishads*, several millennia before our era. Aurobindo thus, startlingly, discovered that the fathers of India's ancient spiritual tradition, the Vedic Rishis, had themselves aspired to transforming the subconscious: they had searched for "the Great Passage" in order to deliver mankind from its invisible servitude. At the dawn of humanity, they had already been seeking for the keys of a human transformation.

Aurobindo had thus taken his first steps in the footprints of the Vedic Rishis, retraced the course of his legendary ancestors. From his arrival in Bombay seventeen years earlier with the revelation of the Atman to this discovery, now, of the first Vedic attempts, everything had fallen into place: he must take up the torch where his great predecessors had left it.

Virtually at the same moment, he again heard the inner voice utter three words within his heart:

"Go to Pondicherry."

Last Days in Chandernagore

In Calcutta, despite police surveillance around his uncle's house in College Square, his cousin Sukumar Mitra (Krishna Kumar's son) had been able to communicate the news and to forward his mail. As to Mrinalini, her life had mercifully been spared more emotional upset. Nivedita had managed to publish four issues of the *Karmayogin*. But Calcutta was rife with the most absurd speculations about Aurobindo's absence. To confront and put a stop to the rumour mill, Aurobindo sent this following tongue-in-cheek "clarification":

> We are greatly astonished to learn from the local Press that Sj. Aurobindo Ghose has disappeared from Calcutta and is now interviewing the Mahatmas [Great Initiates] in Tibet. We are ourselves unaware of this mysterious disappearance. As a matter of fact Sj. Aurobindo is in our midst and, if he is doing any astral business with Kuthumi [who is presumed to have inspired the Theosophical Society] or any of the other great Rishis, the fact is unknown to his other Koshas [sheaths]. Only as he requires perfect solitude and freedom from disturbance for his Sadhan for some time, his address is being kept a strict secret. For similar reasons, he is unable to engage in journalistic works, and *Dharma* has been entrusted to other hands.[98]

Nevertheless, gossips of legal proceedings against him continued to do the rounds. One day, he received a letter from a reader exhorting him to leave his retreat and to confront his judges. This man, a notorious police informer, ironically provided Aurobindo with the opportunity to turn the situation to his advantage.

Aware that his escape through the police net had been a blow to the authorities, Aurobindo retorted that he had no reason to go to court or to leave his retirement since no warrant had been issued against him. Irate, the British government then initiated a new prosecution against him. However, the bureaucratic behemoth was to take weeks to produced a legal warrant – enough for Aurobindo to leave the jurisdiction of British India and begin a new life in the French territory of Pondicherry.

The six weeks in Chandernagore vastly broadened the scope of Aurobindo's inner search. As a sensitive observer, however, Motilal may have been the only person to have detected that Aurobindo's yogic pursuit had now taken irreversible precedence over his political commitment:

> I came away because I did not want anything to interfere with my Yoga and because I got a very distinct adesh [command] in the matter. I have cut connection entirely with politics, but before I did so I knew from within that the work I had begun there was destined to be carried forward, on lines I had foreseen, by others, and that the ultimate triumph of the movement I had initiated was sure without my personal action or presence.[99]

To assist in his departure, Aurobindo knew that he could count on his family's love and devotion, as well as upon the loyalty of his young companions. However, there was no question of unsettling them by divulging his new plans.

The only way to reach Pondicherry, 1,200 miles from Calcutta on the south-eastern coast of India, was to take the maritime route. All road and rail links would be far too risky for a man whose description as a dangerous fugitive was everywhere. A ship of the Messageries Maritimes, the *S.S. Dupleix*, was due to leave Calcutta on the 1st of April and to stop over briefly in Pondicherry on its way to Ceylon. There was enough time to organize the voyage. Aurobindo's cousin Sukumar would arrange two tickets for him and Bijoy (an ex-member of the Maniktala Garden) to be purchased under aliases. Moni, the only boy who was not listed on any police file, would travel ahead by train to the South, carrying a letter from Aurobindo destined for his Nationalist contacts in Pondicherry.

The departure from Chandernagore was scheduled for 31 March. Sukumar had organised the voyage to Calcutta in three stages, with three boats. The final stage would enable the passengers to board the *S.S. Dupleix* from the river, thus avoiding the ship's gangway which was usually under police surveillance. In Bengal which was prey to terrorist violence, two Bengali passengers would not fail to attract unwanted attention.

Unhappily, however, the third boat – with the trunks and tickets – was not at the appointed spot on the river. Aurobindo and his companions were compelled to improvise a hurried trip to College Square (his uncle's house) to retrieve the tickets. As fate would have it, before leaving his native Bengal, Aurobindo's horse-drawn carriage thus drove past the Viceroy's residence in the centre of Calcutta, the headquarters of the British Empire. On that particular day, however, Lord Minto was absent – inspecting India's Northeast Territories and hunting tigers....

Thanks to Sukumar, everything was finally sorted out and the passengers hastened back to the ship with their luggage. But time was now running out to complete one last formality before being allowed to sail: a medical certificate.

At nightfall, as Aurobindo's vehicule with his three companions pulled up to the *Dupleix*, all the passengers had long since retired into their cabins, and the maritime medical officer had left the ship. A coolie proposed to guide them to the medical officer's residence, and so they again drove hurriedly through the European quarter in search of the doctor's home. Anxiety was palpable. What might happen if the medical certificate was unobtainable at this late hour? Aurobindo was silent, "like a man in a trance,"[101] a witness recalled. The doctor delivered the precious certificates without any difficulty, though noticing with some surprise the perfect English accent of one of his visitors.

It was almost 11 pm when the travellers ascended the gangway, where police surveillance had long since disappeared. While Bijoy busied himself with preparing their cabin, Aurobindo's two other companions bade him farewell, bowing silently before him, hands joined in the Indian fashion.

As scheduled, the *S.S. Dupleix* departed at dawn the following day, the 1st of April 1910, navigating through the Ganges Delta and out into the vast open sea, heading south.

Pondicherry

Aurobindo left the political struggle in 1910. In Pondicherry (a French territory), he continued his quest. Like a kind of laboratory of evolution, an Ashram spontaneously developed around him, seeking with him the way to the future of mankind.

Another life had begun. While "the boys" spent their days in town exploring their new environment and learning Tamil, Aurobindo remained alone on the first floor of a house lent by his Nationalist friends. He now had all the leisure to devote himself to his inner research and experience. Time was his own. Or rather, it was pledged to this question: life in a body – for what purpose?

His country had broken the colonial yoke. Through the Nationalist awakening of Swadeshi and Swaraj, India had given an advance notice of her will to the British occupiers, who continued to manage affairs outwardly but had lost the battle of colonialism. It was just a matter of time. As Aurobindo would later clarify: "I knew from within that the work I had begun there was destined to be carried forward, on lines I had foreseen, by others, and that the ultimate triumph of the movement I had initiated was sure without my personal action or presence."[1] Even Gandhi's political blunders would not prevent India from regaining her independence and unity in 1947, albeit damaged by the creation of Pakistan.

Although Aurobindo's remoteness was only apparent and he followed every stirring of his country's life until her liberation, he now cast his gaze beyond India. The world and its future absorbed him. Superimposed in the air, he discerned the delicate cryptograms of terrestrial events (*akasha lipi*),[2] reading the continuum of the human march as if it unfolded before his eyes.

Will the failure of mercantile colonialism sound the final liberation of man, the end of all exploitations? Or are new types of bondage to replace the old ones? Will the global world opening up lead to human unity, or to a fellowship of citizen-consumers whose insatiable appetites demand the global wreckage of the planet? How to stem a scourge which involves every human being and affects the entire earth, but the scope of which we do not yet perceive beyond our personal egoism?

How to change humankind? Change humankind! This was a refrain so often heard. But where was the key to human software concealed?

In the little Pondicherry house, Aurobindo filled his days with intensive activity. He walked back and forth on the terrace for hours; he practised muscular exercises to test the powers of *anima* and tried to free his body from the pressure of gravity. Using philological insights, he immersed himself in the Vedic texts with a view to establishing linguistic parallels between the ancient Aryan civilisation and the Dravidian language. But none of these physical or mental activities disrupted his inner poise; every gesture, every thought remained conscious. Thus, another kind of reality, an emanation of the Infinite, progressively penetrated his body and his mind – transforming them.

The descent of Sri Aurobindo into the origins of corporeal life is an entirely new adventure. A whole volume would be necessary to describe the progression, day after day and for forty years, of a transformation that could open the way to a future humanity reconciled with itself and in harmony with its earthly Mother. Conscious of his divine birth, free from the old phantoms, this human being would be the living answer to: life in a body – for what purpose?

Postscript

What happened to India's Independence Movement and to the participants in the events of these troubled times, after Aurobindo departed British India for Pondicherry?

For the next three decades, *Pax Britannica* continued to reign supreme over the country. The British regime consolidated its sovereignty by exploiting communal divisions between Hindus and Muslims; the political strength of the Muslim League grew, while the Congress remained for a few more years a "politically correct", rubberstamp chamber, dominated by the same "moderate" leaders.

Pherozeshah Mehta (known as "the Lion of Bombay") became a Knight of the British Empire and a member of the Viceroy's Legislative Council; he and **G. K. Gokhale** remained fiercely opposed to the presence of any Nationalist in the Congress. In 1909, after supporting **Morley** in his reforms (Morley-Minto Reforms), Gokhale visited **Gandhi** in South Africa and convinced him to return to India to apply his methods of *Satyagraha* [passive resistance] and *Ahimsa* [non-violence]. Gandhi followed his advice, arriving in India in 1915, and promptly making

Gokhale his political mentor and guide in the halls of Congress. Of Gokhale, Gandhi said: "Pure as crystal, gentle as a lamb, brave as a lion and chivalrous to a fault, the perfection-made man in the political field."* Mehta and Gokhale died in 1915, a few months apart.

Surendranath Banerjee ("the uncrowned King of Bengal") continued to hide his personal ambition behind his Nationalist discourse. Raised to the rank of Knight of the Empire, he gave himself away by endorsing the Morley-Minto Reforms, which were rejected by a vast majority of his compatriots. He ended up discrediting himself in the eyes of the public by accepting a ministerial position in the government of Bengal. His defeat in the 1923 election ended his political career. He died in oblivion in 1925.

In June 1914, coming home after six years' captivity in Burma, **Tilak** returned to work for a Nationalist agenda in the Congress. Deportation had somewhat tempered his revolutionary ardour and he offered his oratorical talents to help England's war effort by recruiting young Indians to fight alongside the British Army. Above all, he wanted reconciliation with the Congress. In 1916, he succeeded in reuniting his Nationalist friends within an integrated Congress – the deaths of Gokhale and Mehta had eliminated the main obstacles to this rapprochement. But the Congress was now in the hands of Gandhi and his non-violence policy. Tilak tried unsuccessfully to convince Gandhi to abandon the aim of absolute non-violence ("Total Ahimsa") in favour of Independence (Swaraj). For the next three decades, Gandhism would guide India's political destiny. Tilak died in 1920.

* Judith Margaret Brown, *Gandhi: Prisoner of Hope*.

On several occasions in this book, it has been emphasized that the ideal of non-violence, as preached by Gandhi, could not lead to a diminution of violence on the ground (the horrific massacres that accompanied the British departure and creation of Pakistan in 1947 provide a tragic illustration). As advocated by Gandhi, "the force of love" generated by non-violence was supposed to stop violence by transforming British riot police and repressive authorities into peace-loving, spiritual channels. It took all his apparent casualness and martyr-posturing charisma to make his compatriots swallow the Christian fable of turning-the-other-cheek as a political strategy of liberation against a colonial power equipped with cannons and machine guns.

When he came out of prison in 1908, **Bepin Chandra Pal** went to England where he lived as an exile until 1911, mingling with Indian radicals and attempting to found a new journal. Returning to India, he participated in Tilak's reconciliation efforts and joined Congress in 1916. But he could not hide his disagreements with Gandhi's policies, which now dominated Congress. He repeatedly tried to warn his compatriots against the separatist ambitions of a politicised Islam and criticised Gandhi's strategies to win Muslim favour to the detriment of Hindus. But his voice was not heard. No longer attuned with a country that had almost entirely joined the Gandhian cult, he found himself isolated, his political voice ignored. He continued to express his disagreement through his writings until his death in 1932.

In 1907, after the break of the Surat Congress, **Lajpat Rai** exiled himself to the United States. He returned to his country in 1919, after the war, and resumed his active participation in Congress politics. He was imprisoned in 1921 for his involvement in protest movements against the government. In 1928, walking peacefully at the head of a silent protest march, he was severely beaten by police and died of his wounds.

To pay for his participation in the Nationalist cause, **Subodh Mallik** was deported in 1908, during the Alipore Trial. He died in 1920, and his beautiful residence in Wellington Square, which had sheltered the first debates against the colonial regime, gradually fell into disrepair. Independent India restored his memory by renaming this square in Calcutta "Subodh Mallik Square" and the street of the former Bengal National College he had financed "Subodh Mallik Road".

Chittaranjan Das, the lawyer who had brilliantly defended Aurobindo at the Alipore Trial, began a political career in Bengal. Nicknamed Deshbandhu (Friend of the Nation), he became involved in the liberation movement as editor of his *Forward* newspaper. Advocating harmony between Hindus and Muslims as well as non-violence, he opposed the extreme methods of Gandhi and lost the presidency of Congress in 1922. He remained in contact with Sri Aurobindo and was one of the very few visitors received in Pondicherry. He died in 1925, following a grave illness.

On his release from prison in 1920, **Abinash Bhattacharya**, Aurobindo's faithful aide-de-camp, joined Chittaranjan Das's political movement and began an editorial career at the magazine associated with that party. Over the years, he became a man of letters and a renowned editor in several media outlets. He died in 1941.

Barin, whose death sentence had been commuted to deportation for life in 1909, was freed from the Andaman Islands in 1920, following a general amnesty. Returning to Calcutta, he tried his hand at journalism, then sought out his elder brother in Pondicherry. He lived there for six years, in the Ashram formed around Sri Aurobindo, before returning to Calcutta, where he resumed a career as a journalist until his death in 1959.

Mrinalini never recovered from the trauma caused by Aurobindo's imprisonment in Alipore. Taking refuge with her parents in Assam, she isolated herself living in a monastic life, ever hoping to be reunited with her husband. Ten years later, in 1919, when material conditions finally made it possible for her to contemplate the long journey to Pondicherry, she succumbed to the influenza epidemic plaguing India and the world and causing a hundred million deaths.

Moni, **Saurin**, **Bejoy**, **Nolini**, Aurobindo's young companions, shared his first years in Pondicherry. Despite the frugality of daily life and the precautions imposed by their status as political refugees, they would eventually adapt to an existence radically different from what they had known in Bengal. Some of them eventually returned to Bengal, while others, like Nolini, became full members of the Ashram.

About the Author

Luc Venet was born in Paris in 1943. At the age of 26, while teaching mathematics, he discovered the existence of Sri Aurobindo, began reading his books and travelled to Pondicherry in South India. Here, he met Sri Aurobindo's long-time spiritual companion, the Mother, who was then 91 years old. From this time on, his life would be forever changed and he set out on a lifelong spiritual quest to try to realize the message of Sri Aurobindo.

In 1972, he was accepted by the Mother to live and work in Auroville, the International Community north of Pondicherry. He worked there in publishing and also built one of the first experimental houses.

In 1977, leaving Auroville for America, he helped Satprem publish the 13 volumes of *Mother's Agenda*. Six thousand pages of conversations in which the Mother describes her efforts of continuing Sri Aurobindo's work in evolutionary research, seeking a new future state of being through a conscious cellular transformation. Luc Venet now lives in southern France.

References

Part I

Epigraph: CWSA, Vol. 20, *The Rennaissance in India*, pp. 6-7.
1. CWSA, Vol. 2, Collected Poems, p. 610.
2. F. Max Müller, *The Upanishads*, p. 363.
3. F. Max Müller, *The Upanishads*, p. 12
4. CWSA, Vol. 35, p. 233.
5. Sri Aurobindo: Archives and Research, April 1990, p. 99.
6. CWSA, Vol. 21-22, p. 313.
7. CWSA, Vol. 1, p. 765.
8. A.B. Purani, *Life of Sri Aurobindo*, p. 328.
9. India Office Records, Kimberley note dated 9 September 1892.
10. Gayatri Devi, *Une princesse se souvient*, Editions Kailash, p. 10.
11. CWSA, Vol. 36, p. 35.
12. CWSA, Vol. 17, p. 402.
13. CWSA, Vol. 6-7, p.19.
14. CWSA, Vol. 6-7, pp. 7-10.
15. Allan Hume, Congress founder, quoted in *Modern India* by B. Chandra, p. 207.
16. CWSA, Vol. 6-7, p. 24.
17. CWSA, Vol. 6-7, pp. 19-21.
18. CWSA, *Collected Poems*, Vol. 2, p. 607.
19. As narrated by his grandson: http://fr.wikipedia.org/wiki/Mohandas_Karamchand_Gandhi
20. Sarojini Ghose, quoted by Girijashankar Raychaudhuri in *Sri Aurobindo*, pp. 107-108.
21. B. Ghose, "Sri Aurobindo ", p. 7.
22. B. Chakrabarti, "Amader Aurodada", p. 776-777.
23. CWSA, Vol. 36, p. 123.

REFERENCES

24 CWSA, Vol. 1, p. 111.
25 CWSA, Vol. 1, pp. 112-117.
26 CWSA, Vol. 19, pp. 36, 95.
27 Minor Robert, *Modern Indian Interpreters of the Bhagavad Gita*, State University of NY Press, 1986.
28 CWSA, Vol. 12, p. 41.
29 CWSA, Vol. 8, p. 62.
30 Dinendra Kumar Roy, *Aurobindo Prasanga*.
31 R. Patkar, *Reminiscences*.
32 *Sri Aurobindo in Baroda*, compiled by Rosham and Apurva, p. 79.
33 CWSA, Vol. 36, p. 58.
34 Nirodbaran, *Sri Aurobindo For All Ages*, p. 26.
35 Dinendra Kumar Roy, Aurobindo Prasanga, p. 31.
36 CWSA, Vol. 12, p. 28.
37 CWSA, Vol. 1, p. 107.
38 CWSA, Vol. 27, p. 220.
39 CWSA, Vol. 1, p. 267.
40 CWSA, Vol. 1, p. 268.
41 CWSA, Vol. 2, p. 247.
42 CWSA, Vol.36, p. 47.
43 CWSA, Vol. 36, p. 47.
44 Krishna Dutta, 2003, *Calcutta: A Cultural and Literary History*, Signal Books, p. 142.
45 CWSA, Vol. 6-7, p. 63.
46 Wikipedia, Indian famine of 1899-1990, http://en.wikipedia.org/wiki/Indian_famine; Laxman Satya, *The British Empire and Famines in Late 19th Century Central India*, University of Pennsylvania Press.
47 SABCL, Vol. 4 (translation from Bengali), p. 351.
48 SABCL, Vol. 4 (translation from Bengali), p. 354.
49 P. Heehs, *The Lives of Sri Aurobindo*, Columbia University Press, p. 54.
50 CWSA, Vol. 12, p. 402.
51 CWSA, Vol. 1, p. 156.
52 CWSA, Vol. 1, pp. 324-25.
53 CWSA, Vol. 1, pp. 330-31.
54 CWSA, Vol. 1, pp. 336.
56 CWSA, Vol. 1, pp. 166-67.
57 CWSA, Vol. 36, p. 147.
58 CWSA, Vol. 36, pp. 145-46.
59 Archives of Baroda State, Sri Aurobindo Archives and Research, April 1977, p. 77.
60 CWSA, Vol. 1, p. 720.
61 Surandranath Banerjee, 1902, *Congress Presidential addresses*, p. 609.
62 CWSA, Vol. 36, p. 70.
64 CWSA, Vol. 6-7, pp. 65-66.
65 Abinash Bhattacharya, « Aurobindo », p. 831.
66 Quoted in Anshu Banerjee, *Smriti Tirtha*, Dipak Gupta Publishers, Pondicherry.
67 CWSA, Vol. 35, p. 14.
68 CWSA, Vol. 2, p. 621.

69 Nirodbaran, *Talks with Sri Aurobindo*, Vol 1, p. 122.
70 CWSA, Vol. 36, p. 46.
71 Gopal, Sarvepalli, *British Policy in India, 1858–1905*, p. 269.
72 Note by Governor Fraser of March 1903 quoted by R. Cronin, *British Policy and Administration in Bengal*, p. 11.
73 Goradia, Nayana, *Lord Curzon: The Last of the British Moghuls*, Oxford University Press, 1993, p. 218.
74 S.N. Sen, *History Modern India*, p. 142.
75 S.N. Sen, *History Modern India*, p. 142.
76 S.N. Sen, *History Modern India*, pp. 140–143.
77 CWSA, Vol. 6–7, p. 71.
78 www.importantindia.com/16138/anti-partition-movement-in-bengal-1905/
79 Lord Curzon, Speech at Dhaka, February 1904, quoted by J. McLane, "The Decision to Partition Bengal in 1905", p. 228.
80 Barindra Ghose, *Sri Aurobindo*, p. 13.
81 Barindra Ghose, *Sri Aurobindo*, p. 34, P.Chandwani, *Sri Aurobindo: A Few Reminiscences*, p. 468.
82 Barindra Ghose, *Sri Aurobindo*, p. 20.
83 CWSA, Vol. 18, p. 385.
84 CWSA, Vol. 28, pp. 256-57.
86 CWSA, Vol. 10–11, p. 128.
87 CWSA, Vol. 6–7, pp. 79–89.
88 Nirodbaran, *Talks with Sri Aurobindo*, p. 499.
89 CWSA, Vol. 35, p. 227.
90 CWSA, Vol. 35, p. 15.
91 As reported by Barindra Ghose, *Sri Aurobindo*, pp. 41–42.
92 CWSA, Vol. 36, p. 107.
93 A.B. Purani, *Evening Talks*, Second Series, p. 200.
94 Nirodbaran, *Talks with Sri Aurobindo*, p. 107.
95 CWSA, Vol. 35, p. 235.
96 SABCL, Vol. 4 (translation), p. 351.
97 SABCL, Vol. 4 (translation), pp. 354-55.
98 S.N. Sen, *History Modern India*, p. 142.
99 *Sanjivani*, 13 July 1906.
100 S.N. Sen, *History of the Freedom Movement in India*, p. 92.
101 S.N. Sen, *History of the Freedom Movement in India*, p. 96.
102 Rajaram Patkar, *Reminiscences*.
103 CWSA, Vol. 17, p. 216.
104 CWSA, Vol. 6-7, pp. 100-103.
105 Dr. Amalendu De, *Raja Subodh Chandra Mallik and his Times*.
106 CWSA, Vol. 36, pp. 255-256.
107 CWSA, Vol. 36, p. 52.
108 CWSA, Vol. 6-7, p. 358
109 Rajaram Patkar, *Reminiscences*.

Part II

Epigraph: *Bhagavad Gita*, CWSA Vol. 5, p. 90.
1. Romesh Dutt, *The Economic History of India under Early British Rule*, London, 1956, pp. v-vi.
2. *Autobiographical Notes*, CWSA, Vol. 36, p. 50.
3. *Aurobindo: Archives and Research*, Vol 15, December 1991, p. 234-237.
4. *Bande Mataram*, CWSA, Vol. 6-7, p. 291.
5. *Ibid.*, p. 291.
6. S. Deb, *Aurobindo as I knew him*, p. 21.
7. *Ibid.*, p. 21.
8. *Report of the National Council of Education*, Bengal (1907-1909), Jadavpur University, Kolkata.
9. *The Indian Nation Builders, Vol. 3*, Mittal Publications, New Delhi, p. 252.
11. Nirodbaran, *Talks with Aurobindo*, p. 106.
12. CWSA, Vol. 28, pp. 333-34.
13. S. Wolpert, *Morley and India 1906-1910*, p. 99.
14. *Bande Mataram*, CWSA, Vol. 6-7, p. 111.
15. *Ibid.*, p. 161.
16. *Ibid.*, CWSA, Vol. 6-7, pp. 109-110.
17. *Ibid.*, CWSA, Vol. 6-7, p. 126.
18. *Ibid.*, CWSA, Vol. 6-7, pp. 114-115.
19. *Ibid.*, CWSA, Vol. 6-7, p. 271.
20. *Ibid.*, CWSA, Vol. 6-7, p. 348.
21. *Ibid.*, CWSA, Vol. 6-7, p. 278.
22. *Ibid.*, CWSA, Vol. 6-7, p. 1108.
23. *Ibid.*, CWSA, Vol. 6-7, p. 171.
24. *Ibid.*, CWSA, Vol. 6-7, pp. 160-161.
25. *Ibid.*, CWSA, Vol. 6-7, p. 203.
26. *Ibid.*, CWSA, Vol. 35, p. 239.
27. CWSA, Vol. 35, p. 373.
28. *Bande Mataram*, CWSA, Vol. 6-7, p. 201.
29. R.C. Majumbar, *Struggle for Freedom*, Bharatiya Vidya Bhavan, 1969, p. 83.
30. Notes of G. Khaparde, 31 December 1906, National Archives of India, New Delhi.
31. CWSA, Vol. 6-7, p. 229-230.
32. Rajendra Prasad, *India divided*, Penguin Books, p. 113.
33. Rajendra Prasad, *India divided*, Penguin Books, pp. 113-114.
34. CWSA, Vol. 3-4, p. 864
35. *Bande Mataram*, CWSA, Vol. 6-7, p. 274.
36. *Bande Mataram*, CWSA, Vol. 6-7, p. 271.
37. *Bande Mataram*, CWSA, Vol. 6-7, p. 174.
38. *Bande Mataram*, CWSA, Vol. 6-7, p. 266.
39. *Bande Mataram*, CWSA, Vol. 6-7, pp. 265-266.
40. *Bande Mataram*, CWSA, Vol. 6-7, p. 267.
41. *Bande Mataram*, CWSA, Vol. 6-7, pp. 294, 296.
42. *Bande Mataram*, CWSA, Vol. 6-7, p. 259.

43 *Bande Mataram*, CWSA, Vol. 6-7, pp. 222-223.
44 *Bande Mataram*, CWSA, Vol. 6-7, p. 220.
45 *Bande Mataram*, CWSA, Vol. 6-7, p. 1106.
46 Upen Banerjee, ' Aurobindo Prasanga ', p. 6.
47 A. Bhattacharya, ' Aurobindo ', pp. 835-836.
48 J. Bannerji, ' Aurobindo Ghose – a Study ', p. 483.
49 N. Dutt, ' My Recollections ', p. 601.
50 Bepin Chandra Pal, Indian Nationalism: Its Personalities and Principles.
51 Government of India, Home Department Proceedings, July 1907.
52 *Autobiographical Notes*, CWSA, Vol. 36, p. 56.
53 *Bande Mataram*, CWSA, Vol. 6-7, p. 634.
54 *Bande Mataram*, CWSA, Vol. 6-7, p. 376.
55 *Bande Mataram*, CWSA, Vol. 6-7, pp. 354-55.
56 *Bande Mataram*, CWSA, Vol. 6-7, p. 348.
57 *Bande Mataram*, CWSA, Vol. 6-7, p. 238
58 *Bande Mataram*, CWSA, Vol. 6-7, p. 239.
59 *Bande Mataram*, CWSA, Vol. 6-7, p. 370.
60 *Bande Mataram*, CWSA, Vol. 6-7, p. 395.
61 *Bande Mataram*, CWSA, Vol. 6-7, p. 470.
62 *Bande Mataram*, CWSA, Vol. 6-7, p. 398.
63 *Bande Mataram*, CWSA, Vol. 6-7, p. 515.
64 *Bande Mataram*, CWSA, Vol. 6-7, p. 516.
65 *Bande Mataram*, CWSA, Vol. 6-7, p. 402.
66 *Bande Mataram*, CWSA, Vol. 6-7, p. 613.
67 *Indian Patriot*, reprinted in *Bande Mataram* weekly, 25/8/1907.
68 Rabindranath Tagore, *Namaskar,* translated from Bengali by Kshitish Chandra Sen.
69 CWSA, Vol. 6-7, p. 655.
70 CWSA, Vol. 36, p. 81.
71 *Bande Mataram* case records, published in *Bande Mataram* of 29 September 1907.
72 Dilip Kumar Roy, *Sri Aurobindo to Dilip*, Vol. II, p. 129.
73 *Bande Mataram, CWSA* Vol. 6-7, p. 672.
74 *Ibid.*, p. 770.
75 *Ibid.*, p. 794.
76 Nevinson, *The New Spirit of India*, p. 226.
77 Sri Aurobindo, Letters to Mrinalini (translation), *Op. Cit.*, pp.356-57
78 Barindra Ghose, *Sri Aurobindo as I Understand Him*, p. 46-46
79 *Early Cultural Writings*, CWSA, Vol. 1, p. 650.
80 *Letters On Himself and The Ashram*, CWSA Vol. 35, p. 244.
81 *Letters On Himself and The Ashram*, CWSA Vol. 35, p. 244.
82 *Ibid.*, p. 249.
83 *Letters On Yoga-I*, CWSA Vol. 28, p. 384.
84 *Ibid.*, p. 249.
85 Nirodbaran, *Talks with Sri Aurobindo*, Vol.2, p. 953.
86 Nirodbaran, *Talks with Sri Aurobindo*, Vol.2, p. 953.
87 *Collected Poems*, CWSA Vol. 2, *Nirvana*, p. 561.
88 Sri Aurobindo, Letters to Mrinalini (translation), *Op. Cit.*, pp.355-56
89 *Letters On Himself And The Ashram*, CWSA Vol. 35, p. 260.
90 *Savitri*, CWSA, Vol. 34-34, p. 576.

REFERENCES

91 Anshu Banerjee, *Smriti Tirtha*, p.68.
92 Nirodbaran, *Talks with Sri Aurobindo, Op. Cit.*, Vol.2, p. 954.
93 Nolini Kanta Gupta, *Reminiscences*, p.28-31.
94 Nirodbaran, Talks with Sri Aurobindo, *Op. Cit.*, Vol. 1, p. 39.
95 SACBL, Vol. 4 (translation), p. 351.
96 *Bande Mataram, CWSA* Vol. 6-7, p. 309.
97 *Essays On The Gita*, CWSA Vol. 19, pp. 381-82.
98 *Ibid.*, p. 381.
99 *Ibid.*, p. 28.
100 *Ibid.*, p. 26.
101 *Bande Mataram, CWSA* Vol. 6-7, p. 95.
102 *Essays On The Gita*, CWSA Vol. 19, p. 37.
103 *Bande Mataram, CWSA* Vol. 6-7, p. 585.
104 *Essays In Philosophy And Yoga*, CWSA Vol. 13, p. 30.
105 *Ibid.*, pp. 381-82.
106 *Ibid.*, p. 381.
107 *Ibid.*, p. 386.
108 *Bande Mataram, CWSA* Vol. 6-7, pp. 1071-72.
109 *Ibid.*, p. 1056.
110 *Ibid.*, p. 1056-57.

Part III

Epigraph: *Essays on the Gita*, CWSA, Vol. 19, p. 37
1 *Karmayogin*, CWSA Vol. 8, p. 5.
2 Sri Aurobindo, *Bengali Writings, Tales of Prison Life*, p. 289.
3 Sri Aurobindo, *Bengali Writings, Tales of Prison Life*, p. 289.
4 *Ibid.*, pp. 290-91.
5 *Ibid.*, pp. 292-93.
6 *Ibid.*, pp. 292-93.
7 *Ibid.*, p. 291.
8 *Ibid.*, p. 292.
9 *Ibid.*, p. 292.
10 *Ibid.*, p. 295.
11 Sri Aurobindo, *Bengali Writings, Tales of Prison Life*, p. 293.
12 *Ibid.*, pp. 261-62.
13 *Karmayogin*, CWSA Vol. 8, pp. 5-6.
14 *Essays On The Gita*, CWSA Vol. 19, pp. 132-33.
15 Letter from Fraser to Minto, 19 May 1908, *National Archives of Scotland*.
16 Sri Aurobindo, *Bengali Writings, Tales of Prison Life*, p. 295.
17 *Ibid.*, p. 298.
18 *Ibid.*, pp. 298-299.
19 *Ibid.*, pp. 303-4.
20 *Ibid.*, pp. 295-96.
21 *Ibid.*, p. 312.
22 *Letters On Himself And The Ashram*, CWSA Vol. 35, p. 181.

23 Sri Aurobindo, *Bengali Writings, Tales of Prison Life*, pp. 277-78.
24 *Ibid.*, pp. 318-19.
25 *Invitation* (composed at Alipore), CWSA, Vol. 2, p. 201.
26 Compiled from the memoirs of Sudhir Sarkar, one of the Alipore defendants, in Anshu Banejee, *Smriti Tirtha*, op. cit.
27 *Bande Mataram*, CWSA Vol. 6-7, pp. 1145-46.
28 *Karmayogin*, CWSA Vol. 8, p. 9.
29 A.B. Purani, Life of Aurobindo, *op. cit.*, pp. 113-14.
30 SACBL, Vol. 26, pp. 226-27.
31 A.B Purani, *Evening Talks*, 2nd Series, *op. cit.*, p. 208.
32 A.B Purani, *Evening Talks*, 1st Series, *op. cit.*, p. 139.
33 Nirodbaran, Talks with Aurobindo, *op. cit.*, p. 136.
34 *Karmayogin*, CWSA Vol. 8, p. 8.
35 *Ibid.*, p. 7.
36 Home Secretary Stuart, Government of India, HD-A, October 1909, N° 230-48, p. 3.
37 Chittaranjan Das, The Alipore Bomb Case, p. 107.
38 Manoj Das, *Sri Aurobindo in the First Decade of the Twentieth Century*, Sri Aurobindo Ashram Trust, 1972, p. 124.
39 *Autobiographical Notes*, CWSA Vol. 36, p. 263.
40 Stanley Wolpert, Tilak and Gokhale, New Delhi, Oxford University Press, 1961, p. 219.
41 Manoj Das, *Sri Aurobindo in the First Decade of the Twentieth Century*, p. 137.
42 Rash Behari Gosh, quoted by E. Major, *Viscount Morley and Indian Reform*, p. 69.
43 *Karmayogin*, CWSA, Vol. 8, p. 118.
44 *Ibid.*, p. 9-10.
45 *Ibid.*, p. 3-12.
46 *Karmayogin*, CWSA, Vol. 8, p. 22.
47 *Ibid.*, p. 24.
48 *Ibid.*, p. 27-28.
49 *Ibid.*, p. 19.
50 *Record of Yoga*, CWSA, Vol.. 10, pp. 33-35.
51 *Letters On Himself And The Ashram*, CWSA, Vol. 35, p. 322.
52 *Letters On Yoga-IV*, CWSA, Vol. 31, p. 81.
53 *Karmayogin*, CWSA, Vol. 8, pp. 38-41.
54 *Record of Yoga*, CWSA, Vol. 10, p. 35.
55 Government of India, Home Department proceedings, series A, October 1909.
56 Morley to Minto, 7 July 1909, Morley Papers, India Office Records.
57 *Karmayogin*, CWSA, Vol. 8, p. 365.
58 *Ibid.*, p. 30-31.
59 *Ibid.*, p. 92.
60 *Ibid.*, p. 150.
61 *Times of India*, 31 August 1909; Government of India, Archives of the Home Ministry, October 1909; *Morley Papers*, 5-8 August 1909.
62 *Karmayogin*, CWSA Vol. 8, p. 144.
63 *Ibid.*, p. 208.
64 Government of Bengal, confidential file from the political department 250/A of 1909, p. 4.

REFERENCES

65 *Karmayogin*, CWSA Vol. 8, p. 224.
66 *Ibid.*, p. 233.
67 Article from *India (Tamil Weekly)*, 18 September 1909.
68 *Ibid.*, p. 286.
69 *Ibid.*, p. 304.
70 *Karmayogin*, CWSA Vol. 8, p. 289.
71 *Ibid.*, p. 305.
72 *Ibid.*, p. 278.
73 Sri Aurobindo's Action (February-March 1976), p. 4.
74 J. MacDonald, *The Awakening of India*, p. 49.
75 Manoj Das, *Sri Aurobindo in the First Decade of the Twentieth Century, op. cit.*, p. 160.
76 Manoj Das, *Sri Aurobindo in the First Decade of the Twentieth Century, op. cit.*, p. 143.
77 *Karmayogin*, CWSA Vol. 8, p. 225.
78 Excerpts of a letter by Nivedita to S.K Ratcliffe, 21 July 1909, cited by S. Basu, *Letters of Sister Nivedita*, p. 986.
79 SACBL, Vol. 26, p. 379.
80 *Sri Aurobindo: Archives and Research*, December 1983, p. 105.
81 *Karmayogin*, CWSA Vol. 8, p. 372-74.
82 *Ibid.*, p. 375.
83 *Ibid.*, p. 173.
84 *Ibid.*, p. 331.
85 *Ibid.*, p. 331.
86 *Ibid.*, p. 382.
88 *Ibid.*, p. 440.
89 *Ibid.*, p. 432.
90 *Ibid.*, p. 439.
91 *Ibid.*, p. 443.
92 *Ibid.*, p. 444.
93 *Ibid.*, p. 431.
94 R.C. Majumdar, *Struggle for Freedom*, Bharatiya Vidya Bhavan, 1969, p. 83.
95 *Ibid.*, p. 465.
96 Motilal Roy, *My Life's Partner*, p. 178, 181, 200.
97 *Ibid.*, p. 201.
98 *Karmayogin*, CWSA Vol. 8, p. 461.
99 *Letters On Himself And The Ashram*, CWSA Vol. 35, p. 26.
100 *The Synthesis Of Yoga*, CWSA Vol. 23-24, p. 616.
101 Anshu Benerjee, *Smriti Tirtha*, Dipak Gupta, Pondicherry 2012, p.167.

Postscript

1 *Letters On Himself and The Ashram*, CWSA Vol. 35, p. 26.
2 Motilal Roy, *My Life's Partner*, p. 200.

Printed in Germany
by Amazon Distribution
GmbH, Leipzig